REMAKING
VIRGINIA
POLITICS

REMAKING **VIRGINIA** POLITICS

PAUL GOLDMAN

THE
History
PRESS

Published by The History Press
Charleston, SC
www.historypress.com

Front cover: The Virginia Civil Rights Memorial and Governor's Mansion.
Back cover: Governor L. Douglas Wilder with the author.

First published 2022

Manufactured in the United States

ISBN 9781467151122

Library of Congress Control Number: 2021949219

To Herbert Goldman, Leslie Goldman and Sylvia Goldman

CONTENTS

1. Keeping the Big Boys Honest: The Campaign That Changed
   the Virginia Democratic Party   9
2. The Virginia Democratic Party and the Voting Rights Act   23
3. The Last of the Byrd Machine: Democrats Learn
   Black Politicians Matter   28
4. Edie Harrison Breaks the Glass Ceiling:
   The 1984 Senate Race   38
5. Not a Miracle Worker: Virginians Vote for the
   Best Candidate in 1985   48
6. Doug Wilder's Pathbreaking 1989 Campaign
   on Women's Rights   60
7. The Rainy Day Fund and the Best-Managed
   State Government   77
8. An Outsider Becomes Party Chair: A Free White Man
   Confronts the Virginia Way Mindset   89
9. VMI's Equal Treatment of Women   101
10. Richmond's Elected Mayor Law   105
11. Youngkin's Close Win: White Backlash and
    Black Paternalism   125
12. The Great Equalizer: The Fight for Public Education   132

Notes   151
Index   155
About the Author   160

1

KEEPING THE BIG BOYS HONEST

The Campaign That Changed
the Virginia Democratic Party

It all started forty-five years ago, though at the time, I didn't realize the Virginia Democratic Party was finally moving into the twentieth century, purged forever, at least at the statewide level, of its segregationist roots and its discrimination against women, northerners and even those with a Brooklyn accent. I did not come to Virginia to make history. Truth is, I should not really have been here at all.

My intention in the summer of 1976 was to get my doctorate. I had been working for the State of New Jersey's small but potentially powerful consumer agency. The head of the agency was a brilliant and telegenic Naderesque lawyer whom I liked working for and booking on New York City television stations. Our office was in Newark, a Path Train ride from Manhattan under the Hudson River. New York's TV stations were notorious for refusing to go to Trenton to cover the governor. New Jersey had no network station, and our news barely made it onto city airwaves. But the stations were willing to send their reporters to Newark or at least meet us on their side of the Hudson.

Consumer news had become big in the Big Apple. I thought my boss Jenny Long should run for governor. She had that "it" thing, I thought, in terms of political image. The governor's aides whom I knew from his campaign complained she was getting more facetime across northern New Jersey than he was. All true—I admit I got a kick out of it. She became sufficiently well known to be nominated to the New Jersey Supreme Court, and my friends tell me she proved to be a great chief justice.

But as the saying goes, by the summer of 1976, I had run that rabbit into the ground. I was living with a girlfriend in Manhattan. I missed housesitting in Princeton as I had done for one of the professors. I already had a master's degree in public administration. Dean Campbell had wanted me to get the doctorate. On a whim, I called him in the spring and said I was ready to go back to school. He called back a few days later and said everything had been set: I would be going to the top school, in his view, full scholarship. No application, no GRE, no transcripts, not even a photograph. Everyone in the field knew he had that kind of pull.

I had written a piece on Bobby Kennedy and later gone to work on his presidential campaign. Dean Campbell liked the piece, though he saw more in me than I saw myself. I could have finished the doctorate in two years and had the thesis already written in my head. It would explore the difference between how Democrat and Republican presidents viewed their roles as head of a national administration. I wrote about it in the *Richmond Times-Dispatch* many years later.

A few months later, a formal letter from the University of Michigan arrived. By then my situation and the course of my life had changed.

———

HENRY HOWELL HAD LONG aspired to be Virginia's first non-segregationist Democratic governor. No person opposing the segregationist elements of the party had ever been nominated, but the times were a-changin'. The segregationist Byrd Machine no longer controlled the Democratic Party, but a stultified old guard remained to prevent what it considered to be Howell's radicalism from taking over their party.

What made Howell a radical? What didn't? He supported the Equal Rights Amendment, the Civil Rights Acts, due process, labor unions, a fair wage and equality of opportunity in education, economics and political rights. Worse yet, from the perspective of the aristocracy, was that he could be counted on to keep his promises.

Howell was a brilliant lawyer and former state senator and lieutenant governor who used the courts to help break down discrimination in civil rights, consumer protection and elections. Senator Harry Flood Byrd Sr. was dead, but the General Assembly remained controlled by conservative Democrats due to their seniority and bloc power. Howell had several political allies, but they were more focused on getting elected to the House of Representatives and U.S. Senate, where their legislative power would be attenuated. Howell had his sights set on the Governor's Mansion in Richmond. This made him the most dangerous radical in the state.

By the summer of 1976, he had run four times for statewide office. He had never received a majority of the votes but did win the lieutenant governor campaign in 1971. The upcoming Democratic gubernatorial primary was in June 1977 in advance of November general elections. No expert on Virginia politics believed Howell could become governor. He had run the last two times as an independent, believing the Democrats would never nominate him.

Even Republican analysts were certain that two-term Democratic attorney general Andrew Miller was a shoo-in. The old guard backed him. The polls showed Miller beating Republican lieutenant governor John Dalton by a landslide. Except for labor unions, almost all of Howell's past major contributors were either willing to support Miller or stay neutral. He could count on unlimited campaign funds to stop Howell; by now even Howell's largest financial backers believed the mantra that Howell was too liberal: "This is Virginia, after all," as they told me.

At least Miller was not a segregationist. I always thought Andy to be a decent guy whose political stances were opportunistic, not ideological. He was not against progress or progressivism. He did not seem to have a passion for anything except power. Back then, it was considered politically dangerous for anyone with statewide ambition to be seen as too anxious for progress. This had the whiff of liberalism—by *liberalism*, the old guard meant the belief that Black Virginians, women, Jews, the Virginia Education Association, Northern Virginians, transplants from north of the Mason-Dixon line and union members deserved a coequal seat at the table of opportunity. Naderism was bad too: someone like Howell who opposed giving Dominion Energy whatever it wanted (it was called VEPCO back then or, in Howell's terms, the Very Expensive Power Company) didn't understand how things were done in Ol' Virginny.

The old guard had not captured power by accident and well understood the threat from Henry Howell. True, the Virginia Constitution forbids a governor from seeking reelection. How much could one man do in just four years? Quite a bit, if he cares. Moreover, Howell's election would set a dangerous precedent: people actually don't have to play the old guard's game in order to advance up the ladder of politics. Candidates could advocate for what they believed was right. They knew a Governor Howell would inspire others who had never considered the heights a possibility. "There is no army on earth more powerful than an idea whose time has come," to paraphrase Victor Hugo.

By the summer of 1976, Howell knew he had one last chance to be governor. He would need to run in the Democratic primary: another independent campaign would not only lose but also leave his legacy tarnished forever. Moreover, Howell believed the primary winner would become the next governor. He considered presumptive GOP nominee John Dalton to be a political lightweight and just a puppet for the Republican wing of the old guard.

⚬ ⚬

I DID NOT GO looking to be his campaign manager. Other people had served in the role, but the truth is that Henry Howell had always been his own campaign manager and strategist. I had studied the numbers and had my own views on how he would need to run to beat Miller. Despite the polling, there was a narrow path to victory.

Henry had initially asked me to drive down from Princeton to speak to his most trusted supporters from around the state. He wanted to gauge if they were ready for another campaign. The meeting occurred in a Virginia Beach hotel by the ocean. There was not an influence-peddler or phony in the room, nor any campaign folks looking for a lucrative gig. It was like nothing I had ever seen before in politics. They all admired Howell.

None of them liked Miller, but they would have backed him if he won the nomination. The Miller people thought Howell was a sideshow, albeit a brilliant one. They did not think he looked like a governor, and image was especially important to them. I decided to forgo the doctorate and help Howell win.

⚬ ⚬

I AM NOT CUT out for politics as a matter of temperament. Do not get me wrong: I love politics the way Bobby Fischer loved plotting chess moves, the same way a good lawyer enjoys nailing a cross-examination. In hindsight, I should have gone for my doctorate. I do not have the personal drive for power needed to get to the top in American politics. I neither relish glitz and glamour nor the Barnum & Bailey of politics. At the same time, I know that history shows stagecraft is important and may be part of one's innate political DNA.

At heart I am still a VISTA volunteer, the Jewish kid from the suburbs taking the bus from O'Hare to the downtown YMCA for training. I can still see myself walking into the Y for the first time, the lobby full of people I knew had not grown up in my neighborhood, who likely saw me as the chump that I was.

I am still the same kid who went to Mississippi a year later. I became friends with Alonzo and Velma Mosely. When I helped elect an Illinois governor later in life, I stayed with Alonzo and Velma for almost a year in their Chicago townhouse.

He hailed from Meridian, she from Monroe, Louisiana. I remember them telling me not to be the anti-establishment Paul Goldman once we got into the Deep South. It was still unusual for the three of us to be driving together down there, especially when we got into Mississippi. "They are going to peg you as a troublemaker, and us not much better," they said, "especially if we tell them we are VISTA workers."

I remember staying at Alonzo's grandmother's house for two weeks. She and her friends could not have treated me any better. Somehow, they found out I loved coconut cake. Every day, they baked me a new one.

I was shocked to see white and Black people walking on opposite sides of the street. When we went out at night, we went to places where I was the only white person.

Near the end of my visit, Alonzo told me to hop into the car. His grandfather had not been answering the telephone. "It's not like him," he said. So, we got into his Trans-Am and motored to Mr. Mosely's church. We went inside.

The pastor lay on the floor in his office. "I got this pain in my chest," he moaned.

We did what we could and called an ambulance. It arrived quickly, but the driver refused to take Pastor Mosely to the hospital unless he paid cash up front. I started to protest when Alonzo gave me a look. The white driver demanded $300. I will never forget it. Three *hundred* dollars.

"In my drawer," whispered Pastor Mosely. He surely kept the money there for this very type of outrage.

They put him in the ambulance but would not allow either of us to go with him. The ambulance made good time to the hospital. They wheeled the pastor into the emergency room. The doctor worked on him. The pastor stabilized, and they hooked him to some machines and tubes. Half an hour later, they wheeled him down the corridor to a bedroom. But the white orderly parked Pastor Mosely in the corridor outside of a double-occupancy room. "There is a white man in that room," said the orderly. "I can't put him in there." It took another hour before they got a room for the pastor.

"Welcome to the South," Alonzo said. I found out later that James Chaney, Andrew Goodman and Michael Schwerner had spent a night at Pastor Mosley's church.

———◆————◆———

LONG STORY SHORT: I should have gone for the doctorate and taught social activism at a law school. But I did not, even after Howell called me in August 1976 and told me he would need to renege on our deal. He cut my salary in half and would no longer pay my rent.

The deal-breaking did not come as a surprise. Any good campaign manager is going to backchannel his candidate's promises on campaign funding. I had been doing this since taking over the campaign apparatus in the early summer. I went to see a few of his past backers, ostensibly to introduce myself. I was already being called a "Yankee" by the other side and would eventually learn the Miller people had T-shirts printed up to the effect of "What could this Yankee know about Virginia politics?"

I had never been called a Yankee before. I asked Elise Fishman, the campaign staffer closest to Howell and herself a New York native, whether this was normal. "For you," she said with a laugh. "They don't say that about the women." And certainly not about her, as she had lived in Virginia for many years. "You're different," she advised. She said Howell was the only person in the state who would have someone like me run his campaign. She told me my accent marked me as the first real Yankee to play a major role in a statewide gubernatorial campaign. That was interesting given that she was Jewish. "I might like it," she said, "but Robert E. Lee and Stonewall Jackson won't." That went, she said, for a lot of Howell's supporters, who would think he could not find a Virginian to run his campaign.

In those days, there were no campaign finance reports to file. But Howell kept a record of all his donors on a card file that his law secretary helped keep up to date. (Unfortunately, I cannot remember her name after all these years.) She was a key to his success over the years. She was a salt-of-the-earth type and took a lot of abuse, as did Elise, though Howell would always apologize the next day. In that way, he reminded me of what I had read about President Lyndon Johnson.

As I began checking out the history of Howell's political contributors, one fundamental fact became obvious: the bulk of Howell's money came from two sources: labor unions and Jewish businessmen. Virginia had long been one of, if not the, most anti-union states in the country, with the lowest percentage of unionized workers. Howell was actually a labor lawyer and represented unions, a rarity in Virginia.

But his support from Jewish business owners required a more complicated explanation, one Howell refused to accept, at least when I raised it. Yet I knew him to be too smart to reject it completely. The old guard in Virginia viewed Jews as too liberal for their purposes. By and large, Jews in Virginia supported changes to two pillars of old guard power. The first was rooted in its financial structure. Virginia, from its plantation roots, had long operated via a top-down economic model. Economic wealth stayed in the top strata dominated by families with generational wealth, financial institutions created to serve them and major corporations. New money had little sway and less social prestige. The hegemonic social culture effused a magnolia mentality that relegated Black people, women and those not native to the state to second-class status. Howell mentioned to me on several occasions the anti-Semitism of the Byrd Machine. He believed that Jewish financial support came from his being the most pro–civil rights gubernatorial candidate in the history of the Virginia Democratic Party. With Miller the candidate of the old guard, Howell figured he could always count on the same level of support, or more, from his Jewish business donors.

I had come to a different conclusion. Unlike the old guard's donors, the businessmen behind Howell were smaller, retail-oriented entrepreneurs whose companies sold directly to the general public: furniture stores, restaurants, car dealerships, real estate agencies and so on. They were more Main Street than Wall Street.

On the one hand, Henry was right: they were pro–civil rights and thus found the old guard's efforts to deny the average citizen their civil, educational, political and other rights intolerable. But they also had an economic incentive to want an end to the reign of the old guard.

Take Tidewater, the base of Howell's statewide support. One-third or more of all the potential customers for these retail operations were Black Virginians. The anti-Black politics long dominant in Virginia, coupled with its inferior and discriminatory education system, denied potential customers the ability to get good jobs at good wages. If laws could be changed to create the educational and political culture needed to attract economic investment, then those businessmen and women stood to gain financially. As they saw it, being pro–civil rights meant being pro-business.

One by one, longtime supporters started to give Henry the bad news: he could not beat Miller. They did not want him to run. Andrew Miller was no reformer, but neither was he anti-Black or anti-woman. He would not be an obstacle to all progress, though under him progress would be far slower as compared to a Governor Howell. Miller had a huge lead in the polls. He had gone to Princeton and the University of Virginia School of Law. He represented a new generation of Virginians not tied to the old Byrd Machine. Howell could not win, and Miller would be a step in the right direction, they felt. Howell might have their hearts, but Miller had their brains.

In that regard, their position was either selfish or selfless, depending on your viewpoint. Howell had been the greatest progressive force running for Virginia governor in the twentieth century. He was smeared and vilified for daring to challenge the segregationist status quo.

<hr />

MILLER HAD BEEN STRATEGICALLY making sure he had an anti-Howell image among the old guard. Howell's backers in the progressive wing of the party therefore could not abandon him for Miller. They would not refuse to give Howell some money if he ran. Indeed, Miller's campaign did not ask them to show disloyalty: the attorney general merely wanted Howell's financiers to sit on the sidelines or give him as little money as possible. The excuse offered would seem plausible: a divisive primary fight only served to help an unrepentant segregationist Republican governor install his lieutenant governor as successor.

To be fair, Governor Godwin had first been elected as a Democratic segregationist. By the time he took office as a Republican eight years later, he no longer gave the same racist speeches as in his formative days in the Byrd Machine. But Godwin remained the same inside despite his nascent Republican branding. Lieutenant Governor Dalton had opposed the Byrd Machine, but as Howell and others drove the segregationists out of the Democratic Party, Dalton and others were happy to see them find a home with Republicans.

Democrats had long feared Howell might bolt the party and run as a third-party candidate. This could happen if they nominated candidates in a convention. Virginia had a sore loser statute that prevented a candidate from running for a party nomination, losing, and then running as an independent for the same office. But the sore loser law applied only if a candidate had appeared on a primary ballot: it did not stop someone defeated at a convention from running as an independent.

Miller knew Howell would enter a primary, which Miller felt certain he could win easily. This gave him two general strategy options. He could try to co-opt a few issues associated with Howell's progressivism to make him more acceptable to Democrats in the primary and to Howell's supporters in the general. But back in the 1970s, being pro-Howell in any respect was regarded as politically unacceptable by the old guard along with the state's top campaign financiers. Miller therefore made the pragmatic decision to avoid any risk of being tagged as pro-Howell. On all the issues that defined the Howell brand, Miller kept a safe distance.

HOWELL SOON HEARD ABOUT my backchanneling his donors and decided to concede the money crunch. The campaign, by necessity, would be a shoestring affair. Paychecks would lag, and winning would seem impossible. This left me with three choices. I could quit and get my doctorate after all. I could work for the Carter presidential campaign, as they had tried to hire me away from Howell. I discreetly checked, and a contact said the job remained open. Or I could stay with the new terms Henry offered. Howell said he would understand if I left since he had not been able to live up to our agreement.

I had grown to appreciate Howell's courage in fighting a system that needed reforming, and living at Virginia Beach had become comfortable. What made me stay was a conversation with Larry Sabato, who greatly admired Howell. We had talked on the beach not long before he went to England on a Rhodes Scholarship. Larry considered himself a Howell protégé. During the conversation, he told me he did not think Howell had any chance of winning the primary, but he thought Virginia would greatly benefit by Howell running, even in a losing effort. His reasoning made sense, and I was similarly convinced by Elise, as we were secretly dating. I stayed.

There was a sense of history. "He who wields the knife never wears the crown," as the famed adage from English history reads. Howell had been a leader in expanding possibility: there were now Henry Howells in every state. The adage seemed a reason why change proves hard and why almost all who promise great things do not achieve them. If you did not have the commitment to lead the fight, why would you have the commitment to finish it? I always wondered whether I had that kind of courage. If I abandoned Howell, what would that say about me? Not anything good. I could handle Howell losing but not losing my self-respect.

The salary was not great, but I knew Henry would not cut it again. And contrary to everyone else, I thought we could win.

I HAD A SHEET of calculations proving we could win congressional district by congressional district. It should have taken $1 million. In the end, we raised only about $300,000 and were outspent ten to one. But the numbers were clear: we had a narrow but achievable path to a huge upset. It would take a domino effect of unlikely events falling into place.

Soon the lack of campaign money proved a blessing in disguise. It forced us to run the kind of grassroots campaign Virginia had never seen for governor.

Since the path rested on strong numbers from Black voters, I decided to do something that had not been done since Reconstruction: hire a person of color for deputy campaign manager. I was hoping Ron Charity would agree.

When I first mentioned it to Ron, he flatly declined and said that was not how things were done for white candidates here. I was surprised. He had been the perspicacious tennis coach for a seven-year-old Arthur Ashe. Virginia remained a rigidly segregated society then, barely a decade since the U.S. Supreme Court had outlawed Virginia's poll tax. We still had a segregationist governor. Ron's gifted wife, Ruth, had been one of the Virginia leaders for George McGovern and earned a spot on the Democratic National Committee.

I told Ron I needed him in that role. Our strategy had to engage our most loyal constituency. Howell liked Ron and knew that he and Ruth were extraordinary.

We also needed a press secretary. Without hope of money to run sufficient television and radio ads or direct mail, generating media stories would likely make or break the campaign. No one had a sharper mind than Howell when it came to getting press coverage. I could write speeches and position papers. But both of us could be a little too inventive, if you will. We needed a press secretary who could write and keep things from going off the rails.

In January 1977, Jill Abramson showed up. She had worked for both the *Harvard Independent* and *Time* while in college and wanted to help Howell. Jill was my favorite kind of press secretary: she was brilliant and took not much money for a 24/7 gig.

At the same time, I regret to say that I knew Howell did not believe a woman could do the job of press secretary in Virginia. I was never sure of the reasoning; it likely had to do with his view of the state's political reporters. But it did not take a Pulitzer Prize winner to know Jill Abramson could do the job. I cooked up a scheme to get Henry to hire her. Jill was not thrilled about it, but I told her it was the only way. We needed her to win, and I would take the blame, if it came to that.

I told Howell the *Harvard Independent* wanted to do a profile of him and had sent her to do the piece. He sat for a long interview. Jill went back to her apartment and banged out the alleged article. We gave it to Henry. He loved it. Then I told him the truth.

He was not thrilled—let us leave it at that. But the next day, he said, fine, hire Abramson.

Jill naturally proved smarter than all of us and a better writer. She went on to become the first female editor-in-chief of the *New York Times* and one of the nation's top advocates for women's equality.

Several of Howell's top supporters were silently gay. We needed their help promoting Howell publicly. Back then, this situation might be problematic even in a Northeast campaign. We were already the first gubernatorial candidate to be for the Equal Rights Amendment; the Voting Rights Act extension; the right for public employees to bargain; equality of educational opportunity for all; fully implementing *Brown v. Board of Education*; more educational funding; and the use of the gas tax to fund road improvements, thus eliminating the possibility of diverting education money to highways. Howell had been the leading consumer advocate against Dominion Energy (then VEPCO) overcharging customers. Howell also had been an early supporter of Jimmy Carter, whom the old guard considered to be too liberal, and supported the biggest heresy of all at the time, an easing of the right-to-work law.

At some point, how much change can one candidate advocate in the South in the 1970s? Ron and Henry said I worried too much. We had civil rights. *Roe v. Wade* had been decided four years earlier. The ERA battle was heating up. Conservatives vilified Howell as wanting to let police and firefighters strike, leaving muggers to thrive and homes to burn. I could never figure that line of attack, which implied police and firefighters would leave their posts. Virginia politics in 1977 were basically Black, white and green. If you were anti-green—against allowing people to make money— you were done. If you were pro-green, then you could also be permitted some indulgences in creating a fairer Virginia. The trick was to find the edge of the sweet spot between too little advocacy for those hurting and not so much to receive backlash from the more conservative majority.

I felt we could thread the needle in the Democratic primary, but the experts disagreed. They thought Miller would have too much support from the conservative-to-moderate, largely white, anti-Howell blocs for us to overcome with progressive wing support. They predicted a landslide loss for Howell. This did seem nearly inevitable. We had no money to run television ads.

———————

In 1977, President Carter, a Henry Howell fan, sent his consultants to Richmond to offer their services. They arrived with an elaborate plan and filmed some commercials. I came to their presentation late.

"We don't have that kind of money," I informed them. "In fact, we wasted precious dollars on the ad you did produce." They were shocked and said we could not erase a twenty-point polling gap without television. They asked about Sidney Lewis, the founder of Richmond-based Best Products who had given Howell $300,000 in a previous losing effort. But Lewis, like other Jewish leaders, was not going to fund any such Howell blitz this time. He gave Howell his biggest contribution but hedged his bets and wrote a sizable check to Miller as well. Carter's advisors wanted to know the strategy for beating Miller. They despised him for fighting Carter during his own primary.

My strategy, they soon discovered, relied on one medium: telephones. Howell had the volunteers to keep a large phone bank going day and night. We purchased the official voter registration list. These lists could be culled for names and addresses of likely voters. Next, we matched voter data against phone numbers on computer disks purchased from private venders. We further massaged this into a master list of likely voters from key Howell areas.

Carter had used phone banks in Virginia with mixed results. They realized the plan had at least one virtue: on paper, it would be the most efficient use of our available campaign funds. We spent days and days calling people.

———————

In an interview with the *Richmond News Leader* earlier in the year, I predicted Howell would win if the primary turnout stayed below 500,000. (The *News Leader*, now defunct, was the morning daily edition from the company that published the better-known *Richmond Times-Dispatch*.) The polls were predicting turnout in the 600,000–700,000 range, but those projections defied history. The Miller people had sold themselves and the media on an impossible scenario; 500,000 would be by far the greatest turnout in

Democratic primary history. A poll published shortly before Election Day predicted a landslide win for Miller. The *Richmond News Leader* promised to print those predictions on the front page if Howell won. They did and called me a "Yankee" in the headline, the last time I know that anyone got that front-page affirmation in my new state.

I never doubted the math behind my analysis, but others did, which I had been counting on. The media wanted to make us the tired old underdog. So did the Miller campaign and the political establishment. They believed the more they said it, the more likely it would become true.

When newspapers ran stories about the poor attendance at Howell events, the campaign team was outraged, but I was smiling. "There is a huge anti-Howell vote in the Democratic Party against progressivism," I said. "They dislike Howell more than they like Miller. As long as they think Howell is a loser, the less they are likely to come out and vote for Miller." I repeated this reassurance over and over.

Howell won with 51.4 percent to Miller's 48.6 percent, a margin of victory of about 14,000 out of 493,108 votes cast.[1]

───

A FEW DAYS AFTER the biggest upset in the history of Virginia Democratic primaries, Howell fired me. Technically, he offered to demote me, but I could see it coming. People were whispering in his ear, saying I was taking too much credit for his win. Nothing was further from the truth. I was not feeling well on election night and had barely stayed for the victory party.

Howell generously recognized my contribution in his victory speech. He asked me to stay on the campaign in a different capacity and for more money. I declined. Every time I have done anything in politics for the money, it turns out to be something I regret. Besides, it would not have worked. Howell and I had quite different strategies for running against Dalton. We left on strained terms.

When I became state party chairman twelve years later—quite an amazing turn

Henry Howell campaigning.
Library of Virginia.

of events—I made sure he got the recognition that the party had long denied him.

Henry Howell is a giant of Virginia political history. Howell forced Democrats to abandon the white supremacy that had long been the party's legacy. It was an honor to work with him and the gifted campaign team back in 1977. I do think about him, Elise, Ron and Jill now and again. They treated me far better than I treated them, when all is said and done. That is a hard thing to live with for all these years. But the truth is what it is.

When Howell died, I attended his funeral in Norfolk. The speaker of the House of Delegates, his long-term Norfolk nemesis Tom Moss, arrived late, wearing a seersucker suit.

2

THE VIRGINIA DEMOCRATIC PARTY AND THE VOTING RIGHTS ACT

Henry Howell's upset win in the 1977 primary had shocked the Virginia political establishment. Reactionaries in the Democratic Party wanted to prevent his coalition—a unique combination of working-class families largely in the state's urban minority communities and rural white counties—from having this power when the party picked its statewide candidates in 1981. In today's parlance, they wanted to kneecap the progressive wing of the party.

Leadership therefore decided to do away with the primary. They used their muscle to get the Democratic State Central Committee to replace the nominating primary with a convention, something that had never been done even in the heyday of the segregationist Byrd Machine.

Some of us tried to block the Central Committee from ditching the primary. I knew the true goal of the party leaders: to reduce the power of Black voters in the nomination process. The pro-convention forces won rather easily. At that point, the pro-primary forces threw in the towel.

Howell had retired, and I felt an obligation to continue the fight. I had long admired the work of Thurgood Marshall, Oliver Hill, Ruth Bader Ginsburg, Ralph Nader and lawyers like Howell for using the legal process to fight for average citizens who were denied their First and Fourteenth Amendment rights. I had done legal advocacy, but nothing like challenging the establishment of a southern party.

I knew Lieutenant Governor Chuck Robb to be a good man. I knew he would run for governor and would be the first non-segregationist

Democrat to hold that post if elected. I had met with him many months before for dinner at his home in McLean. His wife, Lyndon Johnson's elder daughter, Lynda Bird Johnson Robb, did not know I was vegetarian until I showed up.

I knew Robb would be good for the state if elected. But election at any price? That is not my value system. Taking voting rights from minorities was something I simply could not condone even if that meant fighting alone.

I was not an expert on the 1965 Voting Rights Act, but I had studied Section 5. This provision is considered by legal scholars to be perhaps the most radical voting rights provision ever enacted. It aimed to prevent a state like Virginia, covered by Section 5 on account of the state's continuing anti-Black legal legacy imposed by its 1902 Constitution, from passing new laws that would reverse political gains expected to be made by Black citizens as the civil rights movement grew stronger.

Members of the political establishment in Virginia were not big fans of the Voting Rights Act. I had marched and fought for equal justice in my younger days, but Howell had long been the only Democrat competing at the gubernatorial level to fully and unconditionally support the Voting Rights Act. In the minds of the all-white Democratic leadership, that made him too pro-Black to be governor. The act empowered working-class families of Virginia, long denied their rights, with sufficient voting strength to nominate their hero. If it weren't for the Voting Rights Act, Howell could not have won the 1977 primary. Virginia Democrats, led by Andy Miller, were either explicitly against extending the act when it would soon come up for reenactment or proposed ostensibly "friendly" amendments intended to gut it.

I was seeing a wonderful Norfolk woman, K., who was far more knowledgeable than I on the inner workings of Virginia Democratic Party politics. For some reason, she enjoyed hanging out with me and did not mind listening to me play political chess night and day.

We got talking one night about the primary-versus-convention imbroglio. She knew how the convention process worked in rubber-meets-the-road details and how they could change voting rights. She asked me whether Larry Sabato had written anything about it. He had already established himself as the top state expert on Virginia voting statistics. I should have called Larry or driven to Charlottesville to see him. But I did not. Nor could I find anything written by him on the matter at the Old Dominion University library.

Back then, we did not have the internet. I spread copies of Sabato's previous works on Virginia voting around her apartment. K. put up with me staying up all night for weeks researching if the change from a primary to a convention fell under the purview of Section 5.

In 1980—the Supreme Court killed it in *Shelby County v. Holder* (2013)—Section 5 of the VRA had a "preclearance" provision. The preclearance mandate meant that before Virginia could enforce any change enacted by the General Assembly to any law affecting voting rights, the state needed to get prior approval from either a federal court or the Civil Rights Division of the Department of Justice. Any citizen could challenge such enforcement with the DOJ.

Having reviewed Sabato's research, Voting Rights Act cases and the statistical analysis I used to map Howell's upset victory, K. and I talked it out one night. She sat on the bed as I paced the room like Professor Kingsfield arguing my case. I remember her taking a drag on a cigarette—I wanted her to stop but no luck there—and giving me that look, like: "You aren't Perry Mason, much less Columbo, and surely not John Houseman, so can we lighten the load a little?" All the research and deduction had unearthed a few truths.

Under the Voting Rights Act, I could challenge the failure to preclear the change even though the Democratic Party of Virginia had already set the convention process in motion. It would foment a backlash within the party, but I could do it as a matter of right. Secondly, the intent of the party for mounting the change did not matter, only the result. My legal burden was to prove, by statistical analysis, that the change seemed, as a matter of reasonable deduction, to dilute the power of the minority vote.

This required me to call the Department of Justice. I talked to a lawyer who referred me to various cases and other materials. He asked the basic preliminary question: Was I sure the party had not precleared the change as required?

The Virginia Constitution gives the General Assembly the power to determine the method used by a political party to choose its nominees. The Supreme Court has always held that states had certain inherent power to protect the integrity and fairness of their election systems. As a constitutional matter, this amounts to a delegation of authority from the public government to a private entity, albeit a political party. Virginia would need to preclear any legislation authorizing a political party to change its method of nomination. Otherwise, the government could evade this federal requirement by delegating to a private nongovernment entity knowing said entity would not be covered by the Voting Rights Act. The case invalidating all-white primaries in Texas had established this principle, in my view.[2] A move from a primary to a convention did amount to a change covered by the Voting Rights Act.

But I was dejected. According to the DOJ, as long as the state law delegating the power to the delegates had prior approval one way or another, then Democrats were free to change their nomination process at any time.

"You tried, babe," K. said. But a few days later, I came back home with an impish smile.

"I got this new theory," I said.

K. listened as I paced back and forth. In the 1977 primary, the minority vote was 19 percent of the total vote. The old guard devised the change to a convention to reduce the power of the Howell wing. Since the Howell wing's bastion of support came from minorities, they needed to choose a delegate allocation formula geared to shift delegates from Black areas to growing, suburban white areas. A formula based on Democratic voting history would accurately reflect the strength of minority voting groups, but a formula with a population factor would not.

Since party leaders wanted to reduce the power of Howell's Democratic voters, they chose a delegation allocation formula based half on Democratic votes and half on population. This greatly benefited suburbs around Tidewater, Greater Richmond and Northern Virginia. The Democrats in these places were overwhelmingly white and less numerous than in Newport News, Norfolk, Richmond, Arlington and other cities.

"You don't need to be a rocket scientist to do the math," K. said, citing one of Governor Robb's favorite sayings. Sabato's figures demonstrated that the influence of the minority vote had been cut in half by going to the 50-50 vote–population delegate allocation formula. There had not been any preclearance of a 50 percent dilution of voting strength, nor could there be: if the General Assembly had passed a law that resulted in such a dilution, DOJ would reject it.

No case I could find had ever alleged Section 5 covered internal party rules such as a delegate allocation formula. To me, it seemed a logical extension of the case law.

After days spent typing up my brief on an old Remington, I had the single-spaced missive ready. The next morning, K. drove me in my best suit to the Greyhound station in downtown Norfolk. Once in D.C., I took the Metro to the DOJ. I did not have an appointment. The receptionist sent me to the Voting Rights Section.

Reagan had been elected, but he would not be sworn in until later that month. He had campaigned as an opponent of the Voting Rights Act.

There were no cellphones, so supplicants were left to their own noodling or newspapers. I remember seeing an article asking: Would the Reagan Justice Department enforce the Voting Rights Act?

I believed they would. These were professionals, many living in Northern Virginia suburbs. I did not know any DOJ attorneys personally, but I knew many similarly situated public servants. They were good people who would enforce the law—provided, of course, I could make the case.

In a few hours, a young lawyer from the Civil Rights Division brought me into his office. We talked for a while. I remember him taking notes as I did most of the talking and gesturing. He politely smiled and nodded. I told him that discrimination and vote dilution are simply that: wrong, unconstitutional and banned.

"We will get back to you," he promised.

But DOJ never contacted me by phone or letter. Several months later, K. called me. We were on the breakup side of things, but not totally done.

"Congrats," K. said.

"What happened?" I asked.

"Did you see the paper?"

Owen Pickett, a delegate and old Byrd Machine operative serving as party chairman, and others had been savaging my reputation and character for months. K. had warned me they were vicious; they were even accusing me of being a GOP plant. The usual suspects in the news media, who have spent a lifetime being a conduit for such chatter, parroted the character assassination.

K. said the DOJ had apparently agreed with my legal theory and told the party leadership they could not use their allocation process. A deal had been cut. Democrats promised at least 15 percent of the delegates to the 1981 convention would be minorities. The party promised that if they used conventions to nominate statewide candidates in the future, the formula would be solely based on Democratic voters and not 50 percent based on population.

The media did not grasp the ramifications, nor did I. Four years later, when Doug Wilder became the first Black Virginian to seek a Democratic Party statewide nomination, the delegate allocation formula played a foundational role in his ability to make history.

3

THE LAST OF
THE BYRD MACHINE

Democrats Learn Black Politicians Matter

People often ask me about my collaboration with Doug Wilder and whether I really thought he could be elected statewide. Do I remember when I first told Doug that he looked like a governor, would make a great statewide candidate and could win if given the opportunity? I do. Did he think I had lost my mind? I remember what he said. The conversation came up during a political battle few Democrats know took place. To use today's vernacular, it would be considered a Black Politicians Matter moment.

Wilder used his voice as the lone Black senator in Virginia, spoken on behalf of those locked out, to command, insist, *demand* respect. Henry Howell had started the ball rolling as the point of the political lance taking on the hidebound Democratic elite. He had gifted and energetic support, including the Richmond Crusade for Voters, the state's premier political organization for Black voters, and Delegate "Doc" Robinson in the General Assembly. Howell had harnessed minority support to power an upset win in the gubernatorial primary. But despite an early lead in the polls, he lost badly to John Dalton that November. In politics, to push a movement from hope to power, you need to ultimately have your candidate win an election. Any size victory will do. But you must win.

Four years later, Chuck Robb won the governorship. Wilder helped him, as did I. Wilder and I first met during the Robb campaign. Robb became the first non-segregationist Democratic governor in Virginia and received 97 percent of the Black vote. His victory margin was so large that no single constituency could lay claim to it. Moreover, I knew Robb's top political advisors had been strongly anti-Howell in their political views. They used the term *liberal* the way Fox News uses it: as a dog whistle to say someone was pro-Black, pro-union and un-Virginian. Northern Virginia Democrats were derided as white liberals, as if that were bad. Robb largely flew above this type of politicking. I really do not think he enjoyed political party squabbling; he delegated his lieutenants broad authority in party squabbles. It is equally true that he surrounded himself with advisors who were moderate to conservative.

They did not mind Wilder having a seat at the table, but they considered him a liberal just as Republicans did. Robb's aides feared their chief becoming too beholden to Wilder, which meant Black Virginians, in political terms. Howell had driven the segregationists out of the Democratic Party, but the remnants of the Byrd Machine still saw Virginia as beholden to the white conservative voters, and they were comfortable with consequences flowing from this calculation. Robb himself did not hold that view, but Democrats who did controlled the General Assembly by huge margins. Robb had no incentive to ruffle their feathers.

Robb likely did not give much thought to the 1982 U.S. Senate race until after his January 1982 inauguration. Incumbent Harry F. Byrd Jr., "Little Harry," had been appointed in 1965 to fill the vacancy created after his father succumbed to cancer. The Byrd Machine had ruled state politics from the 1920s until the passage of the Voting Rights Act in 1965.[3] Little Harry was first elected senator as a Democrat in 1966. He bolted the party in 1970 and easily won two more times running as an independent in three-way races. The other senator was Republican John Warner.

After the Democratic sweep in 1981, Robb's advisors were thinking they had the formula for winning in a southern state. Why they choose Delegate Owen Pickett is still a mystery to me. Friends of mine who knew Pickett say he was a decent man and that he was not the type of person to say the kinds of things I heard he said about me during the legal imbroglio over the delegate allocation formula. It is difficult to appreciate Virginia's political climate back in the early 1980s. I was quite the oddity: the southern (New York) accent, my diet (the *Washington Post* used to call me a vegetarian) and my belief that Black candidates could win statewide. That Pickett could not relate to me is a fair way to look at it: we are all products of the society we were born into. In Virginia, people had their place.

Robb's advisors believed they needed a candidate who could run well in the state's growing Republican enclaves. Pickett represented one, Virginia

Beach, in the House of Delegates. Pickett's perceived suburban appeal had made him the Robb team's choice as party chair, though he had flouted their orders in that position.

It struck me as ill-conceived. I did not have direct contact with Pickett, but I talked to people who knew him and liked him. I knew my politics and had studied his record. He was no fan of progressive politics. Nor did he appreciate the growing role of Black Virginians in state politics. During the delegate allocation fight, Pickett had shown himself to be a narrow-minded politician unable to grasp its racial import.

Wilder symbolized new power. But Pickett, like other key players in the Robb orbit, refused to recognize it. In their minds, they ran the state. Wilder might be consulted on the nominee for the Senate, but Robb's inner circle would make the call, and others would need to get in line.

The strategy from the Robb team and Democratic old guard to win Little Harry's seat rested on taking Henry Howell's constituency for granted. Where else could such voters go? Robb's folks knew Senator Byrd had no love for his presumptive Republican opponent, Paul Trible. The young GOP congressman had been brash enough to declare for the Senate race before Byrd had formally announced whether he would seek reelection. Robb's crew believed this gave them an opening to neutralize Byrd. Pickett needed to demonstrate fealty to the Byrd legacy.

What were they thinking? The segregationist Byrd Machine ruined more lives over its five-decade reign than any combination of Confederate generals. For the Black community, indeed for any knowledgeable and remotely progressive Virginian, Byrd was a four-letter word. His son had been a loyal lieutenant and heir apparent back in the day and never shed the contemptible philosophy of his namesake.

Robb understood all this. His advisors did not. Party leadership simply wanted to win at any cost. Pickett had never been a major player in the changes sweeping the state. He was an empty vessel, for better or for worse.

In my view, Pickett did not hatch the plan to praise Byrd. Robb would have told him it was a bad idea. As far as the governor's advisors and party command, none had been a leader in the changes sweeping across the state. They did not understand the full scope of the Byrd legacy, as it had not hurt them. Frankly, though they did not support it, they had benefited from it. Pickett received historically bad advice. But the candidate has the final say, so it is on him in the final analysis.

The Robb crew easily arm-twisted the State Central Committee into choosing a convention. There existed no viable opposition to the governor's handpicked choice. Pickett did not need to campaign, he did not need a platform, he did not need to do press interviews and there were no debates. Even the typical party activist did not know a great deal about Pickett. He was given the nomination. His ability to amass a delegate majority had never been in doubt, and the delegates were legally bound to vote for him on the first ballot. No challenger in modern Virginia history with such a thin record and now broad party support had secured a nomination to the U.S. Senate with this much ease and this little transparency. Delegates did not know their candidate had decided to kiss Byrd's backside.

As Pickett had just become the presumptive nominee, his first press conference drew great attention. To Pickett and Robb's advisors, a show of support for Byrd's "fiscal conservatism" seemed shrewd. Republicans were sure to label Pickett as a wasteful spender, a supporter of big government welfare programs and a sure vote for Democratic deficit budgets. If you did a poll, most voters would say they supported "fiscal conservatism." Pollsters never defined the concept, and I doubt Pickett could except in a thirty-second sound bite, but the attack had the right ring. Politics in Virginia, as elsewhere, is as much about emotion as it is about the facts. Only liberals could be against fiscal responsibility.

Pickett and party leaders believed praising Byrd's fiscal conservatism would protect him from GOP attacks and make him attractive to the Democratic-leaning part of the conservative Byrd constituency. Robb had been careful to cultivate the remaining leaders of the Byrd Machine that had not yet defected to the Republican Party. Should Pickett sway moderates and conservative Democrats on this issue and de facto hold the progressive wing, he could run in the mold that the Robb people believed had won in 1981. In politics, the enemy of my enemy is my friend. Wilder had not been happy, and neither were conservative Democrats with being on Wilder's side. On paper, the strategy may have seemed to make sense, but the reality is it was fatally flawed.

Robb's people did not fully understand the reasons for their 1981 success. Robb had been successful because he was not seen as part of the Howell wing. But Robb did not try to run as a Byrd man: he simply kept Howellism at a distance. Robb needed to tap into those Democratic-leaning voters who had been voting Republican the last three gubernatorial elections. Democrats had just swept the three statewide offices and still had big legislative majorities. Pickett did not need to embrace any part of the Byrd legacy. Why didn't Robb's team and party leaders see that?

They could not see the relationship between Byrd's "fiscal conservatism" and his anti-Black Machine. Byrd did not amass his power merely because he was racist; there were plenty of bigots in Virginia back then, many worse than Big Harry. He did not amass his power due to using labor unions as a bogeyman; there were plenty of anti-union politicians in Virginia back then more vitriolic than he. He did not amass his power due to being a fiscal wizard; there were plenty of politicians in Virginia who could balance a budget, as the public demanded.

None of this made Byrd one of the greatest powerbrokers in American political history, albeit a most deplorable and despicable one. The source of Byrd's inimitable ability to last so long and rule so absolutely was understanding the source of his political power. White rural voters kept the Byrd Machine in power. Byrd used "fiscal conservatism" not as a management principle but as a mechanism to ensure the educational and commercial infrastructure needed to grow the parts of the state opposed to his Machine could not be built. There were more cows than people in Northern Virginia a few decades before Robb was elected. When the Byrd Machine faced Colonel Miller, the greatest challenge to its rule before Howell, several small cities in Southside and Southwest cast more votes than Fairfax County.

Whatever you want to call Harry Byrd Sr., you cannot call him dumb when it comes to knowing the roots and limits of his power. Byrd understood that non-southerners moving to Northern Virginia would never support his politics, nor would the Black population of Tidewater. Byrd realized the more the state grew and educated itself, the less his political and social culture could hold sway. There is a reason white slavers would be punished for teaching enslaved persons to read; it is the same reason the Byrd Machine led southern resistance to the *Brown v. Board of Education* decision outlawing school segregation.

One press conference, one statement, one sentence, one promise of fealty to Byrd's "fiscal conservatism" and Pickett lost the campaign in record time. He would still be the nominee unless he quit the race or released his delegates, but his loss was now a fait accompli. It took several weeks before either Pickett or the Robb team understood the magnitude of their blunder. For the first time in state history, Democratic Party leaders would learn a powerful lesson: Black politicians mattered, and they needed to have an equal seat at the table.

I FIRST HEARD ABOUT Pickett's blunder over WRVA AM radio while driving toward Richmond. There were no cellphones back then. I remember thinking, how can Wilder go along with this? Wilder had always been more pragmatic than ideological in these kinds of situations. Pickett would not be a reliable ally in Washington. Surely Robb, I thought, would get Pickett to take it back, do a mea culpa, grovel if need be. Robb would know something had to be done fast.

I find it hard to believe Pickett truly did not grasp the implications of tying himself to a world-famous segregationist. Perhaps like malaria, one is never truly cured. But maybe that is too harsh a judgment. This was the first speech from someone who lacked the political skills to run statewide. There had been no previous reason to suspect Pickett might admire any part of the Byrd legacy. There would now forever be doubt.

I figured Wilder would play the game and extract a price to give Pickett a second chance. Wilder could threaten all manner of things, even to run as an independent. This had happened in other states over the years, most famously Teddy Roosevelt in 1912, but it never proved the smart move. If Robb insisted on Pickett, no one could stop it.

Robb had gotten 97 percent of the Black vote. His father-in-law was the greatest legislator for Black Americans since Abraham Lincoln. If Robb vouched for Pickett and said the rookie candidate had misspoken, then this would fix it. They would not be shocked that a white Democrat had said something nice about Byrd, and Robb did not need his constituency to love Pickett, merely to vote for him over a Republican. If Pickett did not repeat such foolishness, the incident figured to be forgotten by Election Day.

Wilder played his opening move: either Picket goes, or he would mount an independent candidacy. It seemed the logical negotiating position. The convention loomed weeks away, and every chess game starts with a few moves as each side feels out the board. I never believed Wilder wanted to run; Pickett stepping down would be a hugely successful power play, taking Wilder to a new level of respect and fear in the Capitol. He knew it would mark a watershed in state politics, as did Robb's advisors. Robb and the Democratic leadership did not want to capitulate. Wilder had broken the old rules and laid down a new one: what my constituency thinks matters. To hell with Harry Byrd.

The Democratic leadership still had no intention of treating Wilder as a political equal. Yes, he had power. Yes, he spoke for a powerful constituency. But all Wilder had was an opinion; leadership decided, and the rest fell in line. Leadership resented Wilder's threats to run, which would guarantee Trible's election. Some were even calling his bluff. They figured he would fold, and then they could dump Pickett while wounding Wilder.

I called around, and the consensus was clear: Pickett had to go. We all agreed on the replacement candidate: Lieutenant Governor Dick Davis, who had outperformed even Robb on the 1981 ticket.

At some point I got a call from Robb's press secretary, George Stoddard. Stoddard and I had met during the Robb campaign. I thought he was an outstanding press secretary, but we were not close. It was possible Robb asked Stoddard to ask me to speak to Wilder. They assumed I was working with Wilder on this chess move, but I was not. I got the sense the Pickett people had decided they would not be pushed around by Wilder. Tim Ridley, Pickett's campaign manager, was a good friend of Robb's campaign manager, David Doak.

What spurred the call? My guess is a comment I made in a news story. The reporter interviewed me on Wilder's prospects running as an independent against a Republican and Democrat. I believe we had been talking at the Capitol in the old press area next to the snack bar when I said Wilder would have no chance of winning in a three-way race but he could win a two-way race.

Not long after the Stoddard call, I found a message on my machine from Ruth Jones, Wilder's personal secretary. I have always admired Ruth, who later played an indispensable role in his historic wins. She wanted to know if I would meet with Wilder.

───────

I HAD NEVER BEEN to Wilder's new law office. Construction on the building had not yet been completed. I remember Wilder taking me around to see the progress, explaining the ultimate plans. I recall it being a sunny day. To be honest, I did not give a damn. An office is an office. But I could tell he appreciated art and architecture and was not just some smart politician or lawyer who could afford to buy stuff. I had not focused on that part of him before. After the tour, I remember sitting down in his office at the back of the building.

The following is not verbatim, but I remember the conversation like it was yesterday. Many of the lines I still remember. He sat behind his desk. A newspaper lay there. I sat in a chair directly across from him.

"You went to college, right?" he said.

I laughed. "I did."

"Good college?"

"That's what they say."

"You studied math?"

"I did."

"I hear you are good at math."

"I can add and subtract."

He held up the paper. "Did you see this quote of yours?"

"I read it."

"So, college boy, explain this to me." Wilder asked me how many votes it took to win a three-way race. I answered 33.4 percent. Then he asked me how many votes it would take to win a two-way race. I said 50.1 percent.

"So, college boy, how can it be easier for me to win a two-way race than a three-way race?"

I answered standing up, pacing and gesturing. If you run in a three-way race, you will be labeled as the Black independent. Whether that is fair or not is irrelevant: politics are what they are. I think you will get 80 percent of the Black vote, 30 percent of the white liberal vote and 5 percent of the rest. You will lose big or drop out. This will kill your influence in the party, especially if the Democrat loses. But if you were to get a party nomination in the future, you could count on the party's constituency around the state. "That's why, Senator, I said you had a better chance to get 50.1 than 33.4."

Wilder looked at me for a while. "You think I can get nominated for statewide office?"

"I do," I remember saying. "You look like a potential governor to me," I added. "I have been involved in a few successful races. You are photogenic; you have a good smile. It is an electronic TV game now. You have the experience and the Senate résumé. You can win a nomination, and you can be elected."

This time Wilder looked at me for what seemed an eternity. He said nothing. Then he smiled. "You aren't from Virginia, are you?"

Of course, he knew the answer. But I got the message.

Thinking about the conversation many years later, I realize I was likely the first white person, perhaps any person, to tell him that he looked like a governor and that he could win nomination, not to mention the general. He would have realized the words were sincere. But they must have seemed idealistic mush from someone raised in the North.

Wilder called me a day or so later asking if I would set up a meeting with key groups from the progressive wing. He wanted me to think he intended to run.

I set up the meeting at the Virginia Education Association's headquarters in Richmond. Their top lobbyist, Dick Pulley, was there. There were others from the VEA; I can see their faces but cannot recall their names. Back then, in politics, Dick Pulley was the VEA. He turned it into a political force. He and his wife, Martha, were exceptional people steadfastly dedicated to the cause of better teachers and education, yet both were treated unfairly by many political leaders.

Virginia did not have a true commitment to quality K–12 education, much less the equal educational opportunities required by *Brown v. Board*. I knew Virginia's constitutional pledge to be baloney; Henry Howell first directed me to key writings on the matter. I told Pulley there was no way to truly fix education in Virginia without amending the state constitution to give every child a right to equal educational opportunity. His team's tireless work to put education on the front burner is greatly underappreciated. If the VEA does not have a Pulley Award, it should.

Danny LeBlanc and Russ Axsom from the AFL-CIO were also in the meeting. The Howell allies who led the organization in the Byrd days were gone and Danny and Russ were the aggressive new leaders with a public union focus. We got along great for years. Danny was a real pistol, a strong advocate whom you wanted to have in the trenches. He was a fitness buff who got up early to row the James River. Russ was a Newport News steelworker of the highest integrity who was more laid back and let Danny ride point. Robb and the Democratic establishment tolerated the unions, but they were never equal partners. There were other attendees at the meeting representing progressive groups, but I cannot recall their names many decades later.

As the meeting progressed, it dawned on me: Doug Wilder had never been in the same room discussing statewide politics with these folks, these groups or, to put it bluntly, so many white liberals. The media and the political establishment painted a picture of the progressive wing—minorities, teachers, union members, Northern Virginia liberals—as an organized force. During the Howell campaign, this could seem to be true. But it was not. They just all supported Howell.

Wilder never needed to build a multiracial coalition to win his state seat. He had not faced an opponent since his first victory twelve years prior. The truth was that Black and white liberals had similar goals on civil rights but were not formally pulling the same wagon in Virginia. Pickett had not been the choice of anyone around the table, and their approval had certainly not been solicited.

In theory, even if Wilder lost, he would still be the most powerful Black legislator in Virginia and could protect and help people. But was this true in practical terms? Not really. If Wilder ran as an independent, he would be challenging a Democratic governor and party in a general election. Backing Wilder would therefore expose these people and their organizations to considerable political backlash and repercussions. All these groups needed legislation passed by the General Assembly and signed by Governor Robb.

Wilder never asked me to set up another meeting. He had no graceful way to shelve an independent candidacy, and Pickett would not agree to apologize. Even if Pickett did, it would be too late. At some point, I set up a committee to dump Pickett. Wilder was not involved, but I felt someone needed to say something publicly. It might seem the game was over.

Eventually, Robb accepted reality and Pickett dropped out. The media declared Wilder had taken a big risk and came out a winner. Lieutenant Governor Dick Davis got the Senate nomination but lost the general election to Republican Paul Trible by two points. Wilder had showed he could play hardball at the state level.

4

EDIE HARRISON BREAKS THE GLASS CEILING

The 1984 Senate Race

The name Edythe "Edie" Harrison is barely known today among Democrats. Like Henry Howell, she was ahead of her time and served as the point of the lance driving Virginia forward to respect women as equal political citizens.

A dynamo, Edie was a skilled politician and the driving force behind founding the Virginia Opera Association. Like Howell, her willingness to push for political values drew admirers and detractors. The Norfolk resident had been a Howell volunteer in previous campaigns against the Byrd Machine. We met during Howell's 1977 primary campaign. She usually brought one of her daughters with her.

Harrison was known for an elegant air as president of the Virginia Opera Association that camouflaged a tough activism, particularly on women's rights. The Equal Rights Amendment had emerged as the headline women's issue before the General Assembly, and she made a compelling candidate for elected office. Howell had stepped back from Norfolk politics, which allowed Delegate Tom Moss, a future Speaker of the House, to gain more control over the city's politics. When Harrison decided in 1979 to run for a House of Delegates seat, Tom Moss had become the leading anti-woman lawmaker in the General Assembly.

Moss had come of age during segregation and opportunistically drafted behind Henry Howell and others who fought against the Byrd Machine during the 1950s. He had started out in the 1960s as an anti-Byrd reformer, won election in 1962 and had been allies with Howell. Moss changed as he accrued power. He became arrogant, hostile to progressivism and enthusiastically condescending to women, a retrograde persona that fueled his opposition to the Equal Rights Amendment. Surprisingly, Moss was not a closeted Byrd man: he was a reliable vote for education funding, for example. He was simply an example of, in the vernacular of the time, a male chauvinist. He reputedly liked his liquor, though this could have been conflated with the fact that his legal practice represented clients before the Alcoholic Beverage Control Commission. The state's most respected lawmakers regarded Moss practicing before the state liquor monopoly to be questionable, albeit legal. Moss used racist code words to condemn Wilder. He would often patronizingly say, "That's vintage Wilder," meaning, in effect, "There goes the Black guy again."

Norfolk had seven seats in the House of Delegates, but Virginia did not use single-member districts as it does today. The seven seats were decided in one citywide election. A voter would cast one ballot for one contender, and the top seven won. Nine candidates ran in the 1979 Democratic House of Delegates primary. Despite his growing power, Moss finished third with 12.6 percent of the vote. Harrison ran sixth, getting only 9.7 percent, just sixty-nine votes ahead of the seventh-place finisher. Harrison and the other six Democratic nominees faced a nominal Republican challenge, but all seven cruised to victory. Moss finished second, with 9.5 percent, while Harrison finished fifth and won her first term with 9.1 percent.

I should have seen the inevitable clash coming.

Moss relished his chauvinistic image, a textbook example of a powerbroker flaunting his ability to keep his boot on the neck of women seeking equality. "Tom is an enemy of all women in this state," the legislative director for the Virginia chapter of the National Organization of Women (NOW) once said. Moss's position was not without cost. The Virginia Education Association had long supported Moss because he voted its way on education funding, but by 1980, the VEA and its largely female teachers had moved to a position of not endorsing any anti-ERA candidates. Moss nurtured a grudge against ERA activists and NOW, especially those he derided as "the liberals in Northern Virginia," according to the grapevine.

There was one irony: Moss's top aide was a woman universally respected in the Democratic Party. I never had a sit-down with Moss on the ERA, and I never tried to quiz her about his opposition. I did not know her well, but I believe she backed the ERA. The Virginia Constitution, unlike the federal Constitution, specifically bans discrimination based on sex in Article 1, Section 11.

Moss and Harrison clashed on ethics bills, but few members took ethics seriously. They regarded their seats in the General Assembly as ways to make money and enjoy the perks of power, not to reform toothless conflict-of-interest laws. Virginia legislators met for only a few months per year; they were technically only part-time positions, and the pay was low compared to most other state legislatures. Moss worked to further improve the pay and perks of his colleagues.

Harrison was not willing to kiss Moss's ring. She realized her days in the General Assembly were likely numbered due to impending redistricting, but she earned a reprieve when political infighting held up the overdue switch to single-member districts in 1981. For one final time, all seven Norfolk delegates would be chosen together, but they all would have to run again in 1982 in special elections in newly created single-member districts. Renomination proved easy for both Harrison and Moss. Then Harrison won again in November, running less than 1 percent behind Moss in the general.

For the 1982 elections, the General Assembly, with Moss pulling strings, put Harrison in the same district as a stronger, longtime incumbent she could not feasibly beat. I and a few others suggested she move districts and challenge Tom Moss.

Had she thought about that long before? I did not get that impression, but I assumed it. Virginia does not require delegates to live in their district until being sworn into office. Moreover, voters have never seemed too upset by politicians moving to new districts if they are gerrymandered out. Harrison's situation seemed particularly forgivable since all of the districts were entirely new and there were no true incumbents. Harrison moving into what was ostensibly "Moss's" newly drawn district likely drew more light than heat with voters. It was not a strong reason to support Moss or oppose Harrison.

She and I talked about the campaign many times. She had a path to "Toss Moss," as her campaign button proclaimed. The state's top women's activists offered support and money. If she had asked me to help run the campaign, I would have. But she did not, so I went back to New York and we kept in touch.

It took courage for women to challenge Moss. To use NOW's label, he was likely the most insufferable "male chauvinist" in modern Virginia political history. Moss called her "Edie Amin," which reveals much about him and the climate for a women's activist even in Howell country. African Americans comprised an estimated 25 percent of the vote, and Moss had the endorsement of the city's most influential Black political group. Moss greatly outraised and outspent her. He felt his lead was so secure he could skip grueling door-to-door campaigning day after day. But Harrison knew door knocking could be her secret weapon. She worked so hard she broke her foot and sadly missed seven weeks on the trail. Despite the array of forces against her, Harrison lost by just 509 votes.[4]

With her loss went any chance of Virginia approving the ERA within the time limits set by Congress. Virginia finally approved the ERA in 2020, forty-three years after Henry Howell became the first pro-ERA gubernatorial candidate in state history. There are now enough states to enact the amendment; however, there are difficult constitutional questions concerning whether state ratifications after the congressional deadline are valid.

⊷——⊶

AS A POLITICAL MATTER, John Warner fell into the category of an accidental senator. He ran for the GOP nomination in 1978. His best, though not sole, political asset was his wife, Elizabeth Taylor. If not for Liz, Nixon's ex-Navy Secretary would have been an afterthought at the 1978 Virginia GOP nominating convention.

The GOP had longed for the opportunity to nominate the most popular Virginia Republican, Richard Obenshain. Many Republicans saw Obenshain as a pioneering leader of the Virginia Republican Party. He was a top Reagan supporter before being a Reagan conservative had become avant-garde and then dominant within the GOP.

Obenshain struck me as a thinking man's conservative in a party of two camps: the knee-jerk reactionaries or the former Byrd Democrats. Obenshain had the rare gift of policy and political smarts. He seemed headed for victory in 1978 due to voters' dislike of Carter, which had only grown since the Georgian had carried every state of the former Confederacy except Virginia. No one in the GOP knew voting statistics better than Dick Obenshain, except perhaps his protégé Kenny Kling. While Republicans derided "NOVA liberals" in incendiary mailers, the fact was that Ford's margin of victory in 1976 had come from Northern Virginia. Ford carried not just Fairfax County but even inside-the-Beltway Falls Church while barely losing Alexandria and Arlington.

The Democratic establishment, anti-Howell to a person, were determined to nominate former Virginia attorney general Andrew Miller. He had been the "sure-win" candidate against Howell the year before. Howell's loss in the general convinced the establishment they had been right in the first place. I attended the convention in William & Mary Hall, since renamed Kaplan Arena.

Reverend Pat Robertson still considered himself a Democrat in 1978. His father had been a U.S. senator serving alongside his mentor, Harry Byrd Sr. One of Pat Robertson's disciples was among the half-dozen challengers to the favored Miller. I chatted with Robertson in his RV parked outside the hall. He remembered me from the Howell campaign and was surprised someone with my accent had been able to participate in Virginia politics.

"Not in the ol' days of my father," he reminisced. I replied, "The Byrd guys might not have tolerated you, either." He laughed.

"Miller's got it as long as the opposition is splintered," he ventured. I nodded approval, trying to figure what he might have in mind.

Car dealer and Norfolk city councilman Conoly Phillips was Robertson's preferred candidate. To my knowledge, Phillips had not been an active Democrat. He entered the contest just before mass meetings were held around the state to choose delegates. The usual challengers had not aroused much excitement, so few showed up to vote. He surprised Tidewater committees with a coordinated busing effort. Phillips won outright in several areas and amassed several hundred delegates. This still left him far short of the majority needed to win or even claim leverage in choosing a nominee.

Robertson saw it differently. After I got to my seat in the bleachers overlooking the convention floor, a friend came over to say I might want to slip into a meeting Phillips had called. He had asked the other candidates or their representatives to meet him in the second-floor corner farthest from the podium. I snuck into where they were congregating in an open space behind a mesh screen used to hide construction.

I remember the candidates seated on folding chairs in a circle. Robertson sat behind and to the right of Phillips as I looked at them from across the room. Robertson did all the talking. Phillips had his head down and eyes closed, presumably praying. Unless all the anti-Miller candidates united, Robertson intoned, then the delegates pledged to the other candidates would start moving to Miller and the former attorney general would cruise to victory. If we don't do something, then we might as well go back down to the floor and make it official for him. The reverend's pitch made mathematical sense. Everyone agreed.

Robertson had a proposal: all the other candidates would drop out and urge their supporters to back Phillips. The unstated premise did not require a theology degree. Robertson would not deliver the Phillips contingent to any of Miller's opponents: they would stick with the true believer to the bitter end. Thus, only Phillips had any practical chance of getting a majority since the AG's delegates also had no reason to desert their guy. Miller or Phillips, the reverend never put it that succinctly. But those with any political sense got the message.

It worked as a matter of addition and subtraction. However sensible, it did not comport with the political reality. The other candidates could not back Phillips, much less suggest their delegates join the crusade.

I do not recall anyone else speaking more than pleasantries. I believe Senate Finance Chair Hunter Andrews was the first to leave. He had the best head for figures in the General Assembly, and he knew his and the other anti-Millers' hopes were done. Miller never trailed and won a third ballot victory in the manner Robertson had foreseen. The candidates were set for an Obenshain-Miller showdown. Then the unthinkable happened.

———————

SOURCES SAID OBENSHAIN HAD it locked up against the hapless Miller. I was back in New York jogging at the U.S. Merchant Marine Academy. It had one of the few all-weather tracks in the area, and my mom lived not far from the storied facility. I was trying to get back into long-distance running at the time, and the roads hurt my knees. One afternoon, after finishing up a ten miler on the track—forty laps—I headed for my car.

I opened the door to my Honda hatchback. There were no cellphones, email or internet in those days. After sliding into the front seat, I turned on the radio. Normally, I would turn to one of the burgeoning Big Apple talk shows that presaged Rush Limbaugh. Today, however, I turned to one of the news stations. They were talking about an accident in Virginia with one of the Senate candidates. I frantically began switching channels.

I knew one of Obenshain's regular pilots, Curly Byler, who had also flown Howell around the state. I recall one early morning when we were going to Lynchburg. It was cloudy and misty all the way down to the runway. Curly had learned to trust the instruments, and he was chatting with Howell like it was a day at the beach. Curly was so smooth he may as well have been in a simulator. I remember being disoriented. I knew we were descending—but to what and where? I remember looking through the windshield as Curly landed on an invisible runway. Howell turned toward me and smiled, no sweat. *No way it could be Curly*, I remember thinking.

I landed on another station. Apparently, it had happened the evening before. Obenshain had been flying with a new pilot who crashed at Chesterfield Airport. Obenshain, the pilot and a flight instructor were killed on the night of August 4 as the aircraft was making an otherwise routine night landing.

It was a shock for many. I knew several people close to Obenshain; one has remained a good friend for all these years. Our views on most political issues are far apart, but if I had just one call to make from jail, it would be to him. Richard Obenshain's death was a tragedy.

The Republican State Central Committee had the right under state law to select another nominee. With the traditional Labor Day kickoff for state campaigns quickly approaching, they had to move fast. Obenshain was sui generis, and he had no ready heir apparent; he had been a co-chairman of the National Republican Party, and his profile had long eclipsed any other Virginia Republican. Former governor Linwood Holton, the state's first Republican governor since Reconstruction, had lost badly to Obenshain at the convention. Conservatives warily viewed Holton as a more moderate, Rockefeller Republican than a true conservative in the mold of Reagan or Obenshain.

When the GOP looked high and low, it found only one candidate who could raise the money and mount a statewide campaign on the shortest of notice: John Warner. They had derided him only months ago as a dilettante with a famous wife. Now the World War II and Korean War vet, once head of the navy, seemed to have the only guns big enough to catch the now favored Miller. Only Warner could raise the money and harness the celebrity power important in American politics, a trend that had only accelerated in the age of television. John Warner it was.

Warner proved a much better campaigner than the party pros had imagined. The many-times-divorced Taylor—was it seven or eight times? people joked—became popular on the stump even in conservative areas. Plus, 1978 would turn out to be a blockbuster midterm year for Senate Republicans nationwide.

Miller had a big head start in fundraising and organization, and I recall his staff thinking they had gone from sure loser to certain winner. But once again Miller started with a big lead only to come up tantalizingly short. He lost by barely 0.4 percent, or 4,721 votes. It remains the closest Senate election in state history.

OUT OF TRAGEDY ROSE John Warner to what would prove a widely admired Senate tenure. When his 1984 reelection came around, Warner seemed invincible. He would have the tailwinds of a presidential election year, too. Democrats seemed destined to nominate Carter's vice president, Walter Mondale, easily caricatured as a liberal to Virginia voters. Warner merely had to surf the Reagan landslide wave.

The Democrats had no big gun to challenge him. Lieutenant Governor Dick Davis, the narrow Democratic loser in 1982, intended to run for governor, as did Attorney General Gerald Baliles. Governor Robb had more than a year left in office and no desire to run for the Senate. Had he decided to run, former Northern Virginia congressman Joe Fisher could have counted on establishment backing. Leadership would have seen him as too liberal, but at least he would have been a reliable part of the men's club.

The moderate and debonair Warner had worked hard and adroitly to sweet-talk the Democratic establishment. While leadership would have preferred a Democrat, they were not overly energized about defeating him. Littler guns in the General Assembly were not interested.

As 1984 approached, Edie Harrison had been on the political sidelines for two years. I don't recall precisely when she and I first discussed her running against Warner. I believe I was the first to raise the matter with her, but it is also possible she thought of it on her own and had discussed it with advisors. She did not seem surprised when I mentioned the possibility.

It was true that beating Warner might not actually be possible that year. But no woman had previously been nominated for any statewide office, and this glass ceiling needed to be shattered. Like most Republicans, Warner had been less than eager to be associated with women's issues.

Democrats chose to select their nominee at a May convention. A primary required all candidates to file nomination papers by April, but in a convention, a candidacy can emerge at any time. Harrison announced weeks before the convention officially opened. Harrison had tried to take out Tom Moss only a few years ago. The unprecedented challenge to a member of the club—on women's issues, no less—had not been forgotten. It surely should not be rewarded.

Today much is said about the history of discrimination faced by non-whites and women in the Virginia Democratic Party. Little is said about a more curious statistic: how many times Democrats of the Jewish faith like Harrison have run for statewide office and the equal number of times they have all been defeated. Non-white Virginia Democrats have run for statewide office ten times: Doug Wilder and Justin Fairfax won three times between them. Women have run six times: former attorney general Mary Sue Terry won twice. Jewish Democrats ran for statewide office in 1977, 1981, 1984, 1989, 1996, 2001, 2005, 2006, 2009 and 2021: all were defeated.

In the hidebound analysis of the old guard, Harrison was not merely a woman: she was Jewish and a Howell supporter born north of the Mason-Dixon line. For the convention, Edie had the Democrats' anti-woman wing, anti-Howell wing and anti-Jewish wing aligned against her. She also lacked the resources to mount a truly effective campaign against multimillionaire John Warner. The headwinds were veritably insurmountable. To be fair, Governor Robb and his team equated political success with money. They both doubted Harrison could raise the required funds or that she understood the game at the federal level. They knew the women's movement remained split on her viability and therefore their support for her candidacy.

I stayed at Harrison's house strategizing for weeks in the leadup to the convention. Some female leaders strongly supported her breaking the glass ceiling, even as they brooked no illusions regarding the difficulty in unseating Warner. Harrison had been a progressive force who had the courage to challenge Tom Moss, and some saw securing the nomination as a victory. On the other side were strong female leaders who thought their cause would be set back if Harrison lost. A year later, I would see the same split among key players in the Black community as Wilder's shoestring campaign to win his lieutenant governor nomination loomed over the convention process.

Harrison did not get bullied and did not quit. She was talented, as was her staff. I was happy to be a small cog. I helped with messaging and made some phone calls; I remember sunny days jogging through Norfolk. I do not recall speaking with Howell, who by then was not merely retired but had stopped playing politics altogether.

The establishment kept floating other names, but no one else wanted to run against Warner. Some likely saw Harrison as a sacrificial lamb or had, at least, a better-her-than-me philosophy. Governor Robb later conceded that he had underestimated Harrison as a candidate and as someone who deserved more than perfunctory support after winning the nomination.

A countervailing wrinkle is not well known today: as the convention approached, Robb and his team had found their perfect candidate. He was, at the time, a prominent and massively wealthy member of the Norfolk community. He was a friend of Harrison who could have spent $5 or $10 million on his own campaign. He would mean a huge payday for politicos and the party. Had he shown interest months before, he might have won the nomination. I do not mention his name because he never formally announced. I felt he was being used as a pawn in an anti-Harrison play by reactionary elements in the party. They hid their motives from him; he was not a seasoned political operative and never sought political office. I doubt he thought he could beat Warner. Moreover, his rumored candidacy quickly faded when Harrison refused to get out.

Harrison won an uncontested nomination. She gave a terrific acceptance speech, but that proved the high mark of her campaign. After she won the nomination, Democratic leaders claimed in the press they had never ridiculed her or her candidacy, much less opposed it. Harrison knew that protocol required a public display of party unity. She ran a valiant underdog race against Warner. But she, along with Walter Mondale and Geraldine Ferraro, lost in a tidal wave. Once Mondale promised to raise taxes, I knew the Democrats were doomed. I know the man who convinced Mondale to make the pledge, but since he is deceased, I will leave that to posterity as well.

I failed to appreciate the depth of personal hatred too many in my party felt toward change agents like Howell and Harrison. Years later, I remember going to Howell's funeral. Tom Moss came late, despicably wearing a seersucker suit. The establishment's antagonism toward Wilder and racial minorities is what is most discussed today. But they also feared Wilder, so they would go only so far. They did not fear women like Harrison. They enjoyed holding women back.

In looking back at it, I think Democrats need to face facts: the Tom Moss philosophy of disrespect for women was far more widespread than acknowledged. If it were not so, a person like him would never have been chosen Speaker of the House.

Edie Harrison has yet to be fully recognized for her contribution to bringing the Virginia Democratic Party into the post-segregation age. It takes people like her and Howell willing to challenge the status quo for progress to take root. I had not fully appreciated Harrison's guts in challenging the system back in 1982. Men won the race. But Edie Harrison won the history.

5

NOT A MIRACLE WORKER

Virginians Vote for the Best Candidate in 1985

Dwayne Yancey called me a "miracle worker" in his book on Doug Wilder's lieutenant governor campaign.[5] I am like most normal people: who does not like to be flattered? But the fact is I have never seen myself that way. I did not want the role of campaign manager. It got thrust upon me, and I did not initially use the title once it was.

I did not run the campaign to prove anything about race or religion. I grasped the historic nature of the situation, I knew social culture, I saw what world I was living in—but I ran the campaign for one reason: to win.

I knew from the Howell campaign that the Virginia press was inclined against outsiders. In 1973, the media created a hubbub when a Jewish Richmond businessman gave Howell a big donation though large contributions would not normally cause anyone to bat an eye or were even portrayed as a sign of a campaign's bona fides. Howell's opponent's backers spread the news about the wealthy Jew backing Howell throughout Southside Virginia. I witnessed similar attacks on Edie Harrison. So, I figured: let's play it safe. I was Jewish, vegetarian, iconoclastic. There was already a racial hurdle for the candidate to overcome. He did not need a headache from his campaign manager.

Wilder did not care.

When I came on board, he could not afford a campaign manager. I had agreed to do it for $2,000 a month. I liked Doug and his law partner, Roger Gregory, now chief judge of the U.S. Fourth Circuit Court of Appeals. I liked Ruth, Jackie and Michael Brown and George, Arnold and Lynette.

Then, of course, Doug's son, Larry. He could make you feel good just walking in a room.

I remember some friends calling me the White Shadow, after the TV series in which a white person coached a mostly Black basketball team. I resented that. I treated people like people, and Wilder's staff treated me like a person. What the hell does it even mean to treat someone like "like a white person" or "like a Black person"? It is offensive. I believe in Dr. King's dream. Mrs. and Mr. Goldman raised me that way.

Virginia politics in 1985 was as real as it gets. The state had an openly segregationist governor less than ten years earlier. Mills Godwin had been repackaged as a Republican but was the same racist he had been when he was the last governor elected by the Democratic Byrd Machine.

I figured Wilder could not afford anyone like me for the money he had. What other choice did they have? I needed to get the candidate and the campaign to accept me as I was. If he trusted me, then everyone else would, too. I knew I was a little different than the normal lawyer.

People have told me over the years about Wilder slamming me behind my back. If that is what he thought it took to win, that is fine with me. Harry Truman had it right: if you feel the need for a friend in politics, get a dog. Wilder and I were there to win. Such rumors never bothered me.

We won.

The win had nothing to do with miracles. The reason was breathtakingly simple: neither of us had been raised as a white person in Virginia.

The Jim Crow song lyric "If you're black, get back…if you're white, you're alright" summed up Virginia politics after Howell and others challenged the status quo with lawsuits and campaigns. Before then, it was not even enough to be a white male property owner: you had to possess the "right" type of monied male whiteness steeped in the lore and mannerisms of the Lost Cause. Today, public consciousness is beginning to come to terms with the fact that the 1902 Virginia Constitution, based on white supremacy, disenfranchised nearly all Black Virginians, or 90 percent of the relatively few Black male citizens previously on the voter rolls. But many often fail to mention or realize that it disenfranchised nearly half of all registered white male voters.[6] White men who did not pay esoteric poll taxes or pass arbitrary literacy tests were the "wrong" kind of white.

My most important contribution to helping make that history was that I was Paul, the son of Mrs. and Mr. Goldman. I was not there to learn how to be Black; I did not expect anyone to try to appreciate what it meant to be a Jewish kid from New York. I thought about one thing 24/7: how do we win.

It has been thirty-six years of progress, but many Virginians still do not understand this fundamentally. I was not trying to run a social experiment or diversity training clinic. I was not trying to make a statement about white, Black or any people. I did not see myself as this, that or any of the things others were talking about then or historians might write today. I did and do not care what the *Washington Post* or the *Richmond Times-Dispatch* thought about me or what they felt they saw. Paul Goldman is who he is for better or worse. If people want to write or whisper about my flaws, so be it. If they want to praise me, that is fine, too. I simply want to be accepted as Paul Goldman. That is it.

IN CHESS, YOU PLAY the pieces or they play you. At the beginning, the game is different depending on the color of your pieces, but as the game progresses, the colors do not matter as much as how you play.

I was the guy who had not intended to be Wilder's campaign manager. He never even asked me about running for lieutenant governor. He asked to meet because his first campaign manager was not working out.

I was surprised at Wilder's decision to run. A convention would not be friendly to his candidacy. Based on the VEA headquarters meeting of progressive organizations discussed in chapter 3, I had doubts Wilder could rally that wing of the party. I had no intention of being his campaign manager. I merely promised to find him one.

A white woman campaign manager would be unfairly attacked and demeaned. This was Virginia, in the United States, in the mid-1980s, and I was not a fool. Wilder told me that finding a white manager was not possible because no white person in Virginia would do it. I said he was wrong and that if I could not find him one, then I would do it myself. That is the story of how I became his campaign manager. Mrs. Goldman always told me: no one is better than his or her word, and if that is not worth anything, then neither are you.

The racism among many of the party's leaders ran deeper than they could admit. Byrd-era segregationists were no longer Democrats. By 1977, Howell's gubernatorial primary victory and Robb's successful lieutenant governor campaign had committed the party to a new course. However, white politicians along with reporters, commentators and other mainstream and largely white forces did not understand soft bigotry. They did not realize how being raised in Virginia or wanting to be accepted by the political and social establishment had taught most Virginians, including Democratic leaders, to see the world a certain way.

Most importantly, *they could not see that they saw it that way.* That mindset remains part of the insidious legacy from segregation. Everyone today recognizes the physical hallmarks of segregation but believes they can be like Andy Dufresne in *Shawshank Redemption*, pushing through that sewer of mud but coming out clean on the other side. If only that were true. People's minds can come out freer on the other side, but that is different than being completely free. That mental prison was the reason so many smart and good people were convinced Wilder could not win and parroted the mantra as a foregone truth.

It was an Aristotelian Virginia principle that Blacks and whites were a certain way. Isaac Newton did the most uncomfortable thing he could do to his colleagues: he began to question what Aristotle held to be true about nature's laws and proved it was only because they had been raised to think it had always been true.

Larry Sabato's predictions symbolized the conundrum being faced by the Wilder campaign as I looked to find him a campaign manager. Once dubbed "Dr. Dial-A-Quote" by Robb's office due to the media treating him as the ultimate authority on Virginia politics, the professor had been saying what he believed and further claiming Robb and other top Democratic officials agreed with him.[7] He said that no Black candidate could win statewide—especially not Wilder, whom they considered too liberal. Thus, Democrats risked sinking their statewide ticket if they nominated him.

The governor's press secretary, George Stoddart, put all these thoughts into a single soundbite. When asked about Wilder's chances, he lamented, "This is Virginia, after all." It is not a quote either Wilder or I are likely to ever forget. That was it: "This is Virginia, after all." People were raised a certain way. The white population will not vote for Wilder. Do not blame me. It is what it is.

Except it was not. Moreover, this is no longer a matter of speculation. We know for certain it was not true.

I suppose my agent should be jumping in and saying, "You changed this, Paul. Your strategy did it. You are the miracle worker. Embrace it. Charge $10,000 a speech to explain it."

A good story, but it is not true. I am not a miracle worker. I had only one unique thing to offer: I was not raised in Virginia.

Larry Sabato had been. The University of Virginia's most popular professor started in politics as Howell's protégé. Howell thought the world of

Larry Sabato, and that told me all I needed to know. Sabato wrote Howell's transition blueprint in 1977. I am certain Sabato voted for Wilder. Sabato was a Rhodes Scholar and a legend in the political world, and he has had an astonishing career. He despised the Byrd Machine and saw how its odious apparatus ruined the lives of Black and white Virginians. Sabato would have been one of Wilder's biggest cheerleaders on the grounds that Virginia needed to rip the "No Blacks Need Apply" sign from the door to statewide office. But there was one thing he could not escape. He had been raised as a white man in Virginia.

He grew up in Norfolk and then went to college in Charlottesville, where he led the student government. He started working on Howell's campaigns during his teens and became known as a political expert through his writings on Virginia politics. Sabato had seen Howell fail; he had studied the state's history and talked to governors, editors and reporters who all held him in the highest regard. He was recognized as the leading authority on Virginia's elections when he started to opine on Wilder being unelectable on the grounds of skin color. Sabato could not conceive of Wilder winning election to statewide office. He said Wilder could not win, so be it. This is Virginia, after all.

Sabato knew Virginia election statistics better than anyone, except possibly GOP operatives Boyd Marcus and Frank Atkinson. The Virginia Democratic Party had no one of remotely equal knowledge. Bobby Watson on the Democratic side was very good. He was running the gubernatorial primary campaign of Lieutenant Governor Dick Davis. He told me and aide Mike Brown that the Davis campaign had a poll showing Wilder could not eclipse 40 percent, no matter what. Watson had been a great Howell admirer, but he was raised in Virginia.

I had seen this on the faces of those at the 1982 progressive meeting. I am confident everyone in the room backed Wilder in the voting booth, and they were all good people. VEA's Dick Pulley was a Wilder fan. AFL-CIO's Russ Axsom and Danny LeBlanc's complaint about Doug, if they had any, would have been that he was not progressive enough. That was an accurate assessment from the lens of their and Wilder's respective politics. Yet I could tell—it was written on all of their faces when we talked about the 1982 campaign—they did not for a moment think Wilder could be elected statewide. This is Virginia, after all.

As with Edie Harrison among the women's movement, there was a split among key players in the Black community as Wilder's shoestring campaign to win his lieutenant governor nomination loomed over the convention process. Many, including Henry Marsh, one of the state's leading civil rights attorneys, were adamant against Wilder running. I will never forget Marsh approaching me one day at a party event. I can still see him staring me down. I knew him by his legal reputation and that he had been the first Black mayor of Richmond. He chewed me out for giving Wilder false hope. "Doug can't win. This campaign will only wind up setting back Black progress for decades," he said. Marsh "would back any white person" against Wilder. I have never forgotten those words. Marsh and Wilder were opposing forces in Richmond politics. I later learned he and Wilder had been roommates at law school who returned to Richmond to practice law, but not together. Marsh possibly opposed Wilder on personal, not political grounds. I will let others speak to that.

Four decades later, I still do not think Democrats understood the message that the assumption of unelectability sent to Wilder and his constituency. The Byrd Machine said, "No Blacks need apply." Democrats were saying "No Blacks need apply" because no matter the credentials, it would be pointless to try—indeed, would hurt white Democrats in their pursuit of power. Both views, one from hard racists, the other from decent folks who lamented their conclusion, ended up with the same certain conclusion.

Wilder had characteristics other than the color of his skin. He had more experience than the last five lieutenant governors combined, a fact Robb eventually extolled in a television ad. He had won the Bronze Star for Valor in a firefight with Chinese Communists on a Korean hilltop. Marine Chuck Robb and Navy Secretary John Warner had used their military experience to prove they were qualified for governor and senator. They had laudable records; Wilder's medals demonstrated more heroism than Robb's or Warner's. In the Virginia mindset, it did not matter whether Wilder had won more medals than Audie Murphy. He could not win, no matter what.

Wilder would run for lieutenant governor against GOP state senator John Chichester, an ex-Byrd Democrat with no military experience. In Virginia, being a decorated veteran meant winning over a non-veteran. Wilder would be endorsed by the Fraternal Order of Police. Back then, Democrats begged to have such endorsements since Republicans labeled them in coded language as soft on crime.

Robb and party leadership wanted Democrats to stay in office, not least because it was worth a lot of money to a lot of people. The party's establishment and Robb's inner circle included many delegates besides Tom Moss, Dickie Cranwell, Alan Diamonstein, Al Smith and Chip Woodrum, to name only a handful. They all opposed Wilder. Indeed, Wilder had only eight

Strategizing with Doug Wilder. *Author's files*.

solid backers in the Senate from the party's thirty-two-member majority, in which he also served. They all agreed with Sabato: Wilder could not win.

There is not the slightest doubt in my mind that Sabato never understood the message he was sending. As for the others, except for Robb, I have real trouble giving them the benefit of the doubt considering they all backed Tom Moss. It is inconceivable to me that so many leaders could truly plead ignorance of the basic import to their words.

I tried to convince Democratic leadership, Robb, Sabato and others. I pleaded with them to understand the racism in their message: they were, in effect, telling Black Virginians that they needed to know their place and that the white leadership would eventually decide who is the right Black person to run and when.

They all would concede that Wilder had experience, a war record, campaign skills and the endorsements to win a lieutenant governorship that in reality had no power. The office had a great title, but the job is limited to presiding over the Senate and casting an occasional tie-breaking vote, an anomaly in the then-heavily Democratic body.

Robb, Sabato, reporters like Jeff Schapiro and Margaret Edds, along with many others, made sure Wilder and his constituency got the message: it's nothing personal, but—this is Virginia, after all.

ENTER THE SO-CALLED MIRACLE worker who still needed to find Wilder a campaign manager. Back then, the establishment played hardball just like the Byrd Machine had. They tried to ruin Howell financially, as they had others who dared oppose their hold on power. In the close-knit world of Virginia politics, it was clear the establishment had ensured that Wilder could not hire anyone who could navigate the arcane convention process. I would talk to someone eager to run his campaign whose mood would change the next day. Some candidly told me that they were told working for Wilder would not be a good career move. It was a dead end. Finally, I kept my promise and agreed to run the campaign.

I tried to figure out a path to victory. I learned quickly that I possessed the only talent truly useful that year: I was not obsessed with Wilder's skin color. Everyone else was, except the candidate. This led me to another understanding: my existence bothered a lot of people to no end. They were not just saying that no Black person could win; they were also saying that no white person could think otherwise. They never understood that connection, either.

I remember speaking with Ira Lechner, a brilliant Yale Law graduate and delegate who himself ran unsuccessfully for lieutenant governor. We were having dinner one night, and he questioned the following. Wilder, he said, can advocate for or say certain things, and the white community would shrug it off after being upset for a while. But when Lechner took the same stances, the white community came down on him far harder and longer. He leaned across the booth at the diner and asked me: "Why?" He did not give me any specifics because he did not have to. We were both Jewish.

"You're right," I told him. When it came to Wilder pointing out the unfairness in the state and the refusal of those who know better to fix it, the white community and their leaders knew that Wilder was right. They did not like to hear him say it, so they pushed back, but deep down, every white person with a conscience knew that Wilder was right. They could not blame him for speaking out and for being angry at what is and was being done to the Black community. If the shoe were on the other foot, they would be doing the same and refusing to go gently into that good night.

"But Ira," I continued, "you are white."

True, you are Jewish, so we are not First Families of Virginia whiteness, but we are "white enough," if you get my drift. Even with your degrees, there are restrictions on what you are likely to be able to do in this world, but you can do whatever you want, by and large. The difference between you and Wilder in the establishment white mind is simple: they can forgive Wilder since they know what they have done to Black people. But they see you and feel you should have no grievances. The world's possibilities are open to you and have been opened by the same white community you are blasting as racist and reactionary. To put it another way: Wilder has to speak out, but you have a choice because you were born "white enough." Unlike Wilder, you do not have to be a rabble rouser. People who are "white enough" choose to be civil rights advocates, or a union lawyer, in your case. That is why so many think it is unforgivable: they see you as a race traitor. They had the same choice, but they chose differently and to some degree compromised morally. Your existence is a threat to their identity. Your choices challenge their sense of self, which makes them uncomfortable, and you naturally pick up on their discomfort. The thought that you are right about racism and injustice in the society they created is more threatening to them than the thought that Wilder is right, which, on some level, they accept. His life's work and my daily work was, in the establishment mind, assiduously insisting they had sold out or were bigoted for not realizing Wilder could win.

After Wilder won the nomination, I naively thought the criticisms of him and the campaign would stop. It got even worse. Robb and his aides tried to get me fired. Leading Democrats attacked our campaign publicly. The attacks and vitriol made no sense to me. We had defied the experts to win the nomination. Surely that would convince Democratic leaders that maybe we could win the general election, or at least make a respectable showing. They wanted Wilder to win.

Didn't they?

When the larger truth first hit me, I felt foolish for not seeing it earlier. According to the state's top Democrats, they expected the party's white candidates for governor and attorney general to win in landslides. Gerald Baliles, the gubernatorial candidate, had been running a great campaign, as was attorney general nominee Mary Sue Terry. Like Moss, she opposed the ERA, but pro-choice women Democrats were voting for her anyway. She shrewdly championed a crackdown on drunk drivers in the House of Delegates.

The reason Robb and others were desperate to block Wilder's nomination was because they thought he would get crushed. If he had been white, they would not have minded, but in Wilder they saw one thing. They assumed Black Democrats would vote down the line for the party's ticket and when Wilder got his predicted 40 percent, this meant roughly one out of every three white Democrats would have voted for Baliles and Terry but not Wilder. They feared the national media could offer only one explanation: Virginia Democrats were racist. This would crush Robb's national ambitions. Wilder presented a potential catastrophe that would tarnish Virginia as the capital of American racist politics, and politicians would be hard-pressed to justify their previous praise of Virginia having become a tolerant state. All this would have been avoided if Wilder simply lost the nomination in a fair fight.

The establishment had to peer into the abyss for the rest of the campaign and beyond—unless they could offer a plausible non-racial explanation. They could not blame the Black man. That left them with one choice: blame the campaign.

Now I understand the purpose of the party letter threatening Wilder that if he didn't fire me, then they would be unable to help, as much as they wanted to. They were positioning the narrative to be that Wilder lost because he chose to follow an unhinged, long-haired, vegetarian New Yorker. This was a more plausible strategy than considering that Wilder could win. They also knew Wilder was not going to fire me and let someone picked by Robb and Baliles run the show. Had they really wanted to help or cajole, they would call, not send a letter. The letter had been written for revelation after the loss. Robb and his aides knew Wilder did not react well to ultimatums dating back to the Pickett fiasco. It is clear why it is so damning for them: the premise is Wilder could have won or at least made a credible showing if the Robb people were put in charge, a polar opposite position from what they maintained and deeply believed.

In September came the *Washington Post*'s first campaign poll, which established the lay of the land. It showed Wilder twenty-four points ahead. I told the press that this was absurd. Everyone with knowledge of Virginia politics agreed that the *Post* had gotten it hugely wrong, but contrary to the establishment narrative, he was not twenty points behind. All the attention to the horse race number hid the most important number in the poll: Democrats were not leaving Wilder in droves. There were a small number of defectors, but most would support the ticket. Wilder said I had been right the first time we met: it would be easier to win a two-way race than a three-way race.

One journalist had it right: Dwayne Yancey of the *Roanoke Times*. He took the time to follow us through rural counties in southwestern Virginia. He realized all but a few percent of the white Democrats would vote a straight ticket. Baliles and Terry were powerful candidates, and we were weaker, but only marginally. Dwayne grasped it: rural Democrats might think Wilder was liberal, they may not know anyone like Wilder; some may not even want to know anyone like Wilder—but he was not a damn Republican.

Wilder's rural station wagon tour suddenly made sense to the establishment. I wanted Wilder to go in the real world and show the leaders of Virginia that the people were way ahead of them. Robb and Sabato and others said Wilder should not listen to me because I was either an idealist who did not understand people or an incompetent who did not understand politics.

Overnight, the *Post* poll turned me from fool to genius. I was never either one, of course. I had merely done what seemed obvious. Wilder did the same: he campaigned as a competent, trustworthy guy who would work for you. Since the job is of limited power, a lieutenant governor campaign generally becomes a personality contest. Wilder was a charming guy with a good record who had the immensely popular Robb praising his experience in one of Wilder's two major TV commercials. The other featured an endorsement from the Fraternal Order of Police.

Years later, I remember my wife, Leslie, telling me that she and her friends had originally thought the lieutenant governor was above the governor, the way a lieutenant general has more stars than an ordinary one-star general. I got it. Like most people, she had little time for politics. It seemed sleazy and corrupt—with the exception of her husband and Doug, of course. She was right: it is all noise for most citizens. People use street smarts to sniff out the truth.

Voters knew a Black lieutenant governor candidate had to fight his way up the political ladder and earn it. That helped Wilder in the way Terry being a woman helped her: to the average voter, they had to be competent or exceptional, depending on how the voter viewed politicians, because otherwise they would not have gotten that far. All they wanted was to be lieutenant governor or attorney general, and most voters understood that meant they were below the governor. Most voters could not name who held either job right now. Why did it always have to be a member of the Old Boys Club? Why not give qualified new people a chance? We had faith that the people of Virginia wanted the best man to win.

I remember calling my mom a few days after the victory.

"You made the *New York Times*," she said.

"I saw."

"Your uncle said they were crackers when he went to William & Mary."

"That was a long time ago, Mom."

"They say it is some kind of miracle."

"I just followed your advice: if you treat people with respect, you will get respect."

"My advice is to marry that girl, for gosh sakes."

"I understand."

"You getting married, now that would be a miracle."

"It's complicated, Mom."

"No, it isn't complicated at all. You make it complicated."

"I hear you."

"When it is convenient, you mean."

She had me there.

6

DOUG WILDER'S PATHBREAKING 1989 CAMPAIGN ON WOMEN'S RIGHTS

Given all the articles and books on abortion's role in Wilder's gubernatorial victory, I thought it necessary to revisit various published accounts: Margaret Edds, Jeff Schapiro, Donald Baker, editorial boards, among others. The narrative comes down to this: the abortion strategy proved the winning move, a clever piece of Machiavellian strategy. If not for how Wilder played the abortion issue, we would have lost. As a statistical matter, this is true.

This is why I find it so amusing—and unfair —for the media to cast Mark Warner in the role of saving a floundering campaign. As Warner will tell you, he was not involved in developing the abortion strategy. How could he be? He had no formal role whatsoever in the campaign. The truth is that the abortion strategy was fully developed before I ever heard the name Mark Warner in relation to Wilder's campaign.

Mark and I have worked together closely for years; he ran Wilder's gubernatorial transition, to mention one example. He is smart and did a great job. When he ran for governor in 2001, he tasked me with vetting his platform. It ended up at more than eighty pages, the longest campaign platform in state history and on a page-for-page basis, the least read. As far as I know, I am the only one who read the final version word for word, except perhaps for John Milliken, who served as Wilder's transportation secretary and chair of Warner's transition team.

Warner also assigned me with writing his campaign's finance platform. At one point, he called me to say former governor Holton had read the financial plank and considered it too conservative. "Can we soften it a little?" asked Warner. "Not if you want to win," I responded. But he insisted. I wrote an introductory note for him to sign disclaiming that the platform promises were contingent on what we would find when finally getting a look at the state's financial records given our criticism of incumbent Governor Jim Gilmore's budgetary management. Admittedly, this let us have it both ways. I do not recall if this satisfied Holton, but it did Warner.

But he simply did not formulate Wilder's strategy on the abortion issue, which, as the media narrative continues, won the election. Certainly, if you want to highlight the top policy issue, perhaps the only substantive issue in the campaign, it was abortion. Wilder's coolness under fire won it in the final analysis.

———

IN 1989, MOST DEMOCRATS considered themselves pro-choice, and GOP voters were largely anti-choice; however, there was a significant percentage of Republican women, especially in suburban areas, who disagreed with GOP orthodoxy. *Webster v. Reproductive Health Services* had been argued before the U.S. Supreme Court on April 26 that year. Pundits said it had the potential to discombobulate the public dialogue on abortion. I did not give them any mind on April 26 or thereafter. Abortion rankled major constituencies in every southern electorate, including Virginia's, but abortion policy had not proved a major election issue in Virginia since *Roe v. Wade* in 1973. I knew the anti-abortion vote would play a key role in choosing the winner of the 1989 GOP gubernatorial primary but felt that the issue would lose steam when the general election reached the Labor Day kickoff. I was wrong.

Webster was a difficult case for the court. The 5–4 decision announced on July 3 had many moving parts and a mix of concurring opinions. As a legal matter, it did not do what each side claimed: it did not herald the beginning of the end for *Roe v. Wade*. Each side knew the other was being less than candid, but there was no reason for either to point to the legal realities. Five decades later, *Roe* is still here. As a political matter, the case created such an intense reaction because both sides could use it to rally their troops and raise tens of millions of dollars. That morning, abortion politics in Virginia changed instantly, with the gubernatorial race roughly four months away.

The players were pollsters Dave Petts and Mike Donilon. Both would be involved in Democratic campaigns for decades. At this writing, Donilon serves as senior advisor to President Biden. Our media expert was Frank

Greer, who later worked for Presidents Obama, Clinton, Václav Havel and Nelson Mandela. Our press secretary, Laura Lafayette, is now the CEO of the Richmond Association of Realtors. Then there was me and, of course, Wilder.

Women's issues tended to help Democrats in Virginia, as they did across the country. Those inclined to back Democratic candidates leaned pro-choice; those normally leaning the other way backed Republicans. At the national level, Republicans had turned a pro-choice stance into an "abortion on demand" position. Republicans had swept Virginia while winning the White House rather easily in 1980, 1984 and 1988. But Democrats had swept the three statewide offices in 1981 and 1985. Why should it hurt us in 1989?

The GOP would put out a mailer calling Democrats evil for our abortion stance. We would cry foul, and there would be maybe a week of contretemps. Then it would be over, and the issue would be played out, forgotten except by activists. The fact that it was a deep and polarizing issue of women's rights would still not overcome the tendency of politics to be fought out on more centrist turf.

To me, *Webster* posed this question: could Republicans use it to label us the dreaded "L word"? *Liberal.* Republicans would say those who backed *Roe* or opposed *Webster* believed in abortion on demand. In the popular mind, only Hollywood celebrities and other out-of-touch liberals supported abortion on demand. Swing voters thought there needed to be restrictions.

Republicans had tried using the "L word" strategy on Wilder in 1985, albeit not on abortion. The media would have let them get away with this false attack had Wilder not publicly suggested the word had a racial connotation. Republicans cried foul, led by the *Richmond Times-Dispatch*'s ultra-conservative editorial page. Historically, the *Times-Dispatch* mastered the tactic by using the term as a dog whistle on white Democrats like Howell who were supported by Black voters. The *Times-Dispatch* does not like me to say this now and claims it is not fair to bring up those days. The fact remains that in the 1980s, the *Times-Dispatch* editorial board was among Wilder's strongest opponents. They knew Wilder was no liberal by the standards of American politics, but they understood the charge would stick with Virginia voters for one reason. From what I read of the GOP postmortem after Wilder's unexpected win in 1985, top operatives believed they had lost because Wilder bluffed them out of maligning him as liberal. The operatives were not wrong. They vowed not to make the same mistake twice.

Wilder, they said in 1989, was a flat-out liberal, the biggest liberal ever to run for statewide office in Virginia. And even if the charge were not true, they understood it was a winning strategy to allow us all the time and money needed to disprove it. If they could turn Wilder into a liberal, we would have a tough time winning the election. I saw my job as doing a 1985 repeat: come up with a strategy to make the election hinge on anything else.

Governor Baliles's and now Senator Robb's strategists thought they had the answer. Robb and Baliles were both popular and considered themselves moderate-to-conservative Democrats. They backchanneled that they wanted Wilder to run as the heir to the Robb-Baliles government.

This strategy never appealed to me. Democratic partisans and journalists, sources related to me, thought I refused to do it because of some feud I had with the two men. Our polls simply showed that running as their heirs was a losing strategy. People liked both men, but not enough to elect Wilder. Baliles had raised taxes. If we got roped into defending him, we would lose. Wilder had opposed the Baliles tax increase for political and policy reasons. Less than 50 percent of voters wanted a third term of Robb and Baliles and slightly less wanted a change. The undecideds were nominally Republican. Do the math—either way, we lose. Donilon and Petts agreed. At best we would lose by 5 percent running a third-term campaign. Wilder had been campaigning and knew that without a poll. He had to win this on his own.

———— ·—— ·——— ————

BEFORE *WEBSTER*, I COULD not see a path to defeat the GOP favorite, former senator Paul Trible. It was simple math. Any plausible victory required Wilder winning the First Congressional District by a sizable margin. The district starts in the Eastern Shore, crosses over the Bay Bridge tunnel through Newport News and Hampton, then runs toward Washington through the rural counties snaking up the state's border with Maryland. Trible had represented the district in Congress before winning his Senate seat in 1982. Trible would crush us in his old district. Moreover, he appealed to small-town voters, particularly in Southside. He wisely chose to decline to run for reelection in 1988 and run for governor in 1989 instead of being cannon fodder against the hugely popular Chuck Robb. Trible's primary opponents criticized him for ducking a fight against Robb, but it was the only sensible move. Robb won the 1988 Senate race 71 percent to 29 percent against minister Maurice Dawkins.

In a general election, I figured Trible runs far stronger than either of his primary opponents, Eighth District congressman Stan Parris or former attorney general Marshall Coleman. Parris never had a chance to win the primary. As for Coleman, he presented a fascinating profile. He had name identification and had proven to be a particularly good campaigner. The Staunton native would have likely beat Wilder in 1985, but the remnants of the Byrd Machine prevented him from getting the GOP nod for lieutenant governor that year. However, the 1989 race had different dynamics, and Coleman's positions made him seem the easiest beat of the three. As Coleman had started the primary far behind Trible, his team's strategy had their guy turning hard right at every fork in the road. Coleman had never been reactionary about any issue, but he wanted to win. Thus, the opportunistic Coleman had gone to the right of President George H.W. Bush on abortion. Coleman outflanked his opponents by declaring himself opposed to abortions even in the cases of rape or incest. In a three-way GOP primary contest, being alone while barely keeping your feet inside the marker is a way to get votes.

We watched Trible struggle to stay in front. His team had expected a cakewalk, but Parris and Coleman refused to accede to his coronation. They savaged Trible as his strategists held fire, believing he had a sufficient lead to ride above the attacks. Coleman hammered Trible as a coward for quitting instead of seeking reelection against Robb. I never thought Trible was vulnerable to name calling. I thought his main problem would be his House vote to pass a constitutional amendment granting statehood to the District of Columbia. For a Republican congressman representing a substantial Black population in the First District, it seemed a strategic vote. He knew he would face criticism from Republicans, but it gave him bipartisan credibility with a normally Democratic constituency. But by the time Trible ran for the Senate, he knew better than to repeat the stance in a statewide election. He came out against statehood.

Parris did not care about Trible's new position. The Eighth District Congressman representing the D.C. suburbs and exurbs knew the issue would resonate with Republicans in the area. The biggest negative for Republicans there was not the addition to the Senate of two liberal senators. They would not like that, but the principal issue with D.C. statehood for Northern Virginia residents was that statehood would allow the District of Columbia's politicians the power to impose income and other taxes on Virginia commuters who worked in the district. Parris had no chance of winning statewide given his lack of appeal to rural voters. But he would confound the vote in Northern Virginia.

On primary day, June 13, Coleman surprised the experts by eking out a small win over Trible. The deciding vote, in my mind, had come in Northern Virginia and particularly Fairfax County. Parris ran a statehood ad that crushed Trible, allowing Coleman to finish second and Trible a poor third in the vote-rich area. If you take out the D.C. suburbs, then Trible would have won by a decent margin. We could not have beaten Trible had he been nominated.

———— · ————

THE WILDER CAMPAIGN HAD started running positive name-building ads a week before the GOP primary. I had feared the winner would start by condemning Wilder as a liberal and defining the contest from the start. As it turned out, though Coleman's upset was elating, his campaign had been grueling. He ended the primary in debt and physically spent. Coleman was making the same mistake as the Democratic command in 1985: assuming Wilder could not win. His strategists were raised in "this is Virginia, after all."

Did Coleman's team really think they had it in the bag? Our pollster did a poll soon after the primary. Mike Donilon called with the results.

"Do you want the good news or the bad news?"

"Good news first."

"The polls say we can still win."

"So, what is the bad news?"

"Coleman has locked up 49 percent."

"Looks like we need another miracle," I warily joked.

I wish I could say we chose the abortion issue out of brilliance. But it took no genius to realize that we went abortion or went home on election night. Sure, no gubernatorial campaign had ever been staked on a women's rights issue, especially in the anti-ERA South. We had Jerry Falwell's Moral Majority headquartered in Lynchburg and Reverend Pat Robertson in Virginia Beach. It seemed suicidal to some, perhaps many, politicos.

I wish I could say I made the big money Robb, Baliles, Terry and others paid their top campaign staff, but I took a small salary so everyone else would have to cut back, including Greer on his TV percentage. I figured it would save $1 million over the course of the campaign. We would need it. In that regard, Greer sacrificed the most. I believe he did that in part due to his being a strong advocate of civil rights. Wilder gave him no choice, but still, he did it when few of his caliber would have.

Wilder had earned his opportunity. He never anticipated it would hinge on this issue. Taxes, education, government spending, racial justice, law and order… In his long career preparing for this moment, he would have foreseen any of these as the biggest issue, alone or in combination. But abortion? Never. But we all understood the math driving the equation.

Race versus abortion squared off in the South. I had spent years figuring out how we deal with the former. But abortion? The gods of politics had called an audible, in sports terms.

The issues went together under an equal rights rubric. Men had to stop telling women what to do and the establishment had to stop telling people of color what they could do. I got it—two for one. It was a real brain teaser to develop the perfect framing, but it could work.

I found abortion posed profound moral and intellectual issues. I am not able to say when life begins; my religion teaches that life begins at birth. Thus, for those of the Jewish faith, an abortion is not killing a person. Americans of different faiths have different views. Who is to say one view is more moral than the other? Besides, we are all unique people who start as one cell. If left to develop, the result of one cell is a unique human being. In my view, the decision of whether to seek an abortion cannot be based on government compulsion or government prohibition except in the rarest of cases. I could pretend we had a grand theological debate on the matter. Lafayette had been headed to Yale Divinity School and could have held such a debate. I am not going to claim we arrived at our position after rabbinical soul searching. I had no major legal, political or moral qualms with *Roe v. Wade*. My job was finding a winning strategy for a historic campaign.

The campaign would come down to making the right call on abortion. Wilder and I trusted our pollsters. Greer held the same job with the National Abortion Rights Action League (NARAL) and had intimate knowledge about how the issue fared in focus groups around the country. This would prove to be a double-edged sword.

I asked Wilder to hire Donilon, then a rising star with limited state campaign experience, because of two things. Pat Caddell, President Carter's top pollster, said Donilon was brilliant, and he did not say that about many. Donilon said that in his experience the white percentage of the vote on Election Day would equal only the percentage of white voters who said they were definitely for Wilder. White voters who said they were leaning Wilder or undecided were not telling the truth. I remember thinking that could not be true: even the worst candidate will get at least some of the undecided votes on Election Day. I pressed Mike, but he did not budge. This is the main reason I asked Wilder to hire him. Pat Cadell had been right.

Donilon, Petts and I then agreed to add extra protection against rose-colored glasses. In our polling, we would use a statistical model that purposely set the Black percentage of the projected electorate below what we thought it would be. This meant our polls gave us a few percentage points less of the vote than would otherwise be the case, and Coleman got an artificial bump. We were taking away Black voters—97–3 percent for Wilder—and replacing them with white voters who were going to Coleman 60–40 percent. It also tended to make our projected model slightly more male. In 1985, Black turnout had been less than predicted. Wilder's historic presence had not caused shockwaves. Experts were saying race and abortion in a southern state guaranteed a record turnout. What if they were wrong?

Wilder trusted me with this kind of stuff. I had one overriding obligation: keep him in the game no matter what the conditions on the field. The whole country seemed to be watching. Ten times a day, I would get calls from people who had been waiting to see a candidate like Wilder have a chance at the gold ring. Everyone else could give opinions, could say this or that, brag about what they would do, talk behind your back or in front, write things for the newspaper. If we lost, then it would fall on me and the candidate. As President Kennedy wrote, "Victory has a thousand fathers; defeat is an orphan."

Contrary to what the media has said for more than thirty years, we were never confused on our abortion strategy. The usual suspects urged us to go after Coleman as a flip-flopper on abortion. Coleman had indeed zigged and zagged on the issue over the years, and Donilon and I expected him to tack toward President Bush's position in the general. This strategy never appealed to me. People do not fear a flip-flopper since he or she is not a firm believer in anything. In theory you can reason with a flip-flopper. I believed we had to tie Coleman to the extremists on abortion—to be fair, how I would define extreme.

To win, we needed to turn Coleman into Buzz, the character opposite James Dean in the famed drag racing scene in *Rebel Without a Cause*. They are in two cars a quarter mile from a cliff overlooking the Pacific. The rules are simple: start the car, race toward the cliff and the first one to jump out loses. They eye each other and gun their engines. Dean jumps first, as he realizes Buzz is prepared to cut it too close. But Buzz is not being heroic—he had caught the straps of his leather jacket around the inside doorknob. His only option is to stop the car, but this would make him the ultimate coward.

He stays in the car, trying to unhook the jacket, as the vehicle drives over the cliff and crashes into the water below. I needed people to think Coleman was Buzz on the abortion issue.

I knew Coleman was not a believer in anything but his own ambition. One of his aides, Anne Kincaid, was a true believer. I knew Anne, and we had agreed to disagree on the issue years before. Her support for him in the primary gave Coleman's hard right position credibility. Once past the primary, Coleman backed away from her advice. Kincaid was a political force and died far too young.[8]

Donilon's post-GOP primary poll showed it had not produced any lasting fissures in a party hungry to elect its first governor since 1977. Abortion might have split the 400,000 primary voters, but most other Republican or Republican-leaning voters had paid little attention. This enabled Coleman to lock up his 49 percent. He morphed from afterthought into giant killer, an underdog who now stood between the great liberal and the general treasury.

Our biographical ads run during the GOP primary had been well received. The spots depicted Wilder as a war hero, a hardworking lieutenant governor and a man who had earned the top job. But Greer's original cut highlighting Wilder's humble beginnings as a waiter showed he did not yet understand the race issue. Once pointed out, he learned quickly. Greer proved to be a superb ad maker, and his firm did great work. The ad helped improve Wilder's image with the public, but the 62 percent who had voted for Reagan in 1984 and the 60 percent who had voted for George H.W. Bush four years later still viewed most Democrats as liberals in moderate clothing.

If Coleman went into debt and used the money to tarnish Wilder as a liberal in a two-week blitz of TV ads right after the primary, I believe he would have won without difficulty. Why didn't they do the obvious? They have offered a lot of reasons, yet not the one that seems clear to me. Deep down, his key Virginia strategists never believed a Black man could be elected governor over an acceptable white Republican. They were raised in Virginia, after all. After their loss, they talked about Wilder getting free media, press protection and a double standard Coleman raged about in the last week of the campaign. It is true that state and national press were easier on the Black candidate in this race. Did the Coleman aides really want people to believe being white was a disadvantage in the governor's race?

Coleman had other problems. What, precisely, recommended him to the public? Or what justified his attack saying Wilder was unfit to be governor or rant that no one else who had held the chair ever had such inadequate credentials? The press and other politicians did not disagree in spirit. If

I may speak the plain truth, that would mean all the governors whose major qualification was that they were enslavers committed to writing and maintaining human bondage laws, or later because they single-mindedly supported racial segregation and Jim Crow, were better qualified on a moral basis. Let's understand: Virginia had a line of enslavers then segregationist governors whose qualifiers were they (1) were white; (2) believed Black Virginians deserved only the rights wealthy white male Virginians deigned to give them; and (3) would dedicate their public service to maintaining maximum white supremacy even to the point of treason. According to Coleman and his team, they were morally and intellectually superior to a decorated war hero who was voted one of the state's most effective lawmakers.

Coleman went on a rant in the final week because he could not understand how he was going to lose to a Black person. His team could not comprehend that Wilder had more talent and a better record and had run a superior campaign.

I had no unique skillset for running this campaign. Donilon and Petts knew much more than I about polls. Greer knew much more than I about TV ads. Lafayette knew more about how to talk to the media. I do not know political organizing as well as Michael Brown. I do not write speeches better than others. There is not really anything special I brought to the campaign. True, the candidate trusted me, but that is not a skill. I had one major asset that made me unique: I had more confidence in the fairness of the white voters of Virginia than any white Virginian in politics. I never doubted it. As in 1985, that is what I brought to the campaign.

To some, this made me seem like a near-savant because they were first thinking how they would map out the chess board for the usual—in their minds, white—candidate, then they compensated for what they thought was the Black coefficient. On the chess board, the pieces move the same whether they are black or white. No one raised in Virginia had been able to do it in 1985. I quickly realized they could not do it in 1989. I had to figure out the right way to play the abortion issue. And when I did, it did not matter what skin color anybody had.

WILDER AND I WERE on the same page on the abortion issue. If Mark Warner wanted to discuss an issue in his gubernatorial race, he would call a meeting with a lot of people, hash it out and get a consensus. Wilder did not work that way. We would talk; I would talk to Donilon and Greer; and maybe Wilder would join us, maybe not. He would talk to them, too. We didn't have meetings. We had debate prep, strategy and issue discussions, but not meetings like a Warner meeting. Wilder and I knew instinctively what needed to be done.

Greer wanted to take the straight NARAL line: pro-choice, no restrictions, a women's right to choose is absolute, end of story. At the time, I actually did not realize he was NARAL's media guy. I knew he had worked for NARAL in the past, but I did not know the group remained his major client. It would not have mattered to me. With all due respect to Frank—and he is brilliant at what he does and far more accomplished in the world of politics—I was not going to let his advice override what I knew about the state. I did not care what he was hearing from his crowd in D.C. The NARAL line would not work in Virginia.

I recommended Wilder hire Greer for two reasons. First, he could do a terrific sixty-second bio ad, and we needed a great one to win. Secondly, he had become known for the "Greer Pivot." Greer said that policy disagreements were fine, but we should not do negative attacks on Coleman. Let Coleman go negative first, then pivot.

My initial reaction had been that this might well turn out to be the right choice, but it seemed a risky strategy to allow your opponent to hit first and frame the election's storyline. Conventional wisdom was that if we let Coleman hit first, we might spend the whole campaign on the defensive, refuting charge after charge. I thought Greer's point basically echoed Robb's advice from four years ago: Wilder must avoid being the negative guy at all costs. A good strategy, in theory. I understood Greer's unstated observation: Wilder was too weak with white voters to start a fight with Coleman. The bio ad had helped boost our positive ratings but not enough for that.

Greer convinced me on the merits of his pivot. The more he explained, the more I understood how brilliant it was. The move had proven successful in other campaigns. Let Coleman attack first, on whatever issue, even the smallest item in a mailer. It did not matter. At that point, we would run a major ad chastising Coleman for dirty campaigning and then say he went negative because he didn't want you to know something. It was perfect for our situation. What mattered was whether the media would think Coleman had gone anti-Wilder first.

Greer's Pivot allowed us to constantly keep the abortion issue out there by saying Coleman was making false charges against Wilder because he didn't want voters to learn the truth about his extreme position on abortion. It worked. We branded Coleman as a negative campaigner while hitting him with even harder negatives. Polls showed voters blamed Coleman for the nasty campaign.

Greer got that right, but he had a blind spot on abortion. He did not want to deviate from the NARAL line. This missed the most important political angle. No matter how you massaged the data, the statistics showed that more people opposed Coleman's abortion position than supported ours.

There were three things we needed to do. First, we had to avoid being pigeonholed as favoring abortion-on-demand, which was toxic among swing voters. There was only one way for Wilder to avoid this label. It does not matter if the dog whistle is wrong, which is why they are so potent. Dog whistles are all about the heat, not the light. Greer's advocacy for NARAL's positioning proved right so far as Democratic orthodoxy was concerned: when we deviated from the NARAL line, we got tremendous blowback. The *Washington Post* editorial board hammered us. Which is exactly as we had hoped.

We had come out for a few seeming restrictions on abortion rights. We supported parental consent for minors, the only restriction that really got much attention. Amazingly, at this point, I cannot even recall the other restrictions, and they do not seem to be mentioned in any *Post* articles. I believe one involved the rights of the father. The goal was clear: we will not be the abortion-on-demand liberal.

We scored a political home run when the head of NOW came to Virginia to attack our abortion position. NARAL and NOW were against all restrictions. They brooked no concessions on the right to choose and believed that was morally right. The anti-choice, pro-life groups took the same approach. Both wanted that line in the sand, being firm believers but also very aware hard-line stances helped fundraising.

At the same time, I did have a political issue with NARAL and NOW. *Webster* had put the abortion issue at the forefront of American politics. There are only two states with gubernatorial elections the year after presidential elections: New Jersey and Virginia. New Jersey would have a Democratic landslide in 1989. I was not involved but knew enough to know the predictions were accurate, having worked on a winning gubernatorial campaign there in the 1970s. Democratic Jim Florio had endorsed the NARAL and NOW position, but that wouldn't change the outcome. The pro-choice groups had been waiting for a chance to have their issue front and center to show its power at the polls. Virginia held the only competitive statewide elections that year; however, in their view, Wilder would lose. It made all the political sense in the world: with a sure win in New Jersey, why risk a loss in Virginia? If Wilder did not take the full pro-choice line and then lost, that might actually be politically better for NARAL and NOW.

My strategy and thinking reflected someone who treated women's groups with equal respect in this matter. I understood they were operating the way anyone should run an issue group: no permanent friends, only permanent interests. Their job was to protect the rights of women, and they did not owe Wilder or Virginia's Black community anything. By the same measure, my job was to help overcome centuries of political prejudice. If that meant breaking with groups on the left, then so be it, and if that meant they broke with us, then that's just politics, as well. It was nothing personal.

Greer actually held back running our abortion ad, fearing his NARAL's wrath. Wilder had to order him to run it. I later found out Greer had qualms about airing it until he secretly screened it for NARAL and found they liked our approach. Greer felt pulled in several directions or more. I get that. He should have been up front about it and not waited until his permanent client gave him the okay in secret. Wilder deserved better than that.

Political communication should follow the KISS rule: Keep it Simple, Stupid. We needed a ten-second position, not a law review article. Similarly, our stance on parental consent was more nuanced than what NOW said they perceived. NOW likely felt it was easier to simply reject our view. They said we would lose the election because we did not follow the D.C. line on abortion rights. I did not mind: the more NOW attacked us, the less liberal we looked to swing voters.

Wilder had to be for at least one high-profile restriction. As I noted, it was politics and not theology in deciding what that would be. Most Virginians supported parental consent. At the same time, we would come out as pro-choice. Even though this was the popular position, 10 percent more of the electorate disliked Coleman's opposition to all abortions than supported our pro-choice with an asterisk position. Swing voters felt that being against abortion even in the case of rape or incest stemmed from an extremism that put fervor above compassion when faced with a tragic situation.

To win over those swing voters, I needed them to not dwell on our position but rather obsess over what they considered to be Coleman's extremism. But how to do it?

THE MEDIA WANTED A pro-choice versus pro-life narrative; we wanted mainstream versus extreme. As Sabato pointed out, it seemed impossible.[9] Any poll would say that more Virginians were pro-choice than pro-life, but pro-choice lacks nuance that articulates the mainstream view. The average person has some qualms about abortion at some level. Bill Clinton had the dominant public mindset right: abortion should be "safe, legal and rare."[10] "Pro-choice" does not say "rare" to voters. Saying you are pro-choice does not motivate our target swing voter: anti-Coleman, Republican-leaning or independent women. They needed to have an acceptable alternative and be motivated to vote against Coleman. I did not want Wilder to talk about why we thought abortion was okay: I wanted to talk about Coleman's extreme position. We needed swing-voting women to see Coleman as anti-woman—someone who did not trust women and wanted the government to tell them what to do even in heartbreaking situations.

The proper mix of positive and negative attack took time to develop. The platform would not become make or break until after Labor Day. We did not need to invent the perfect pitch right away, we just needed to lay a marker. Our plan involved carpet-bombing TV screens until Virginians got sick of seeing our abortion ad, threw their shoes at it, called up the campaign and said if we didn't take the ad down, they would vote for Coleman. That is when you know the ad is working.

The real debate in the Wilder campaign occurred in messaging arguments over our abortion ad: the imagery, the words, the right moment to blanket the airwaves. We needed to do three things at once: block the liberal tag, let people know our basic position and force the entire election to hinge on this mainstream versus extreme fault line.

The anti-government, libertarian thesis seemed the only way to do it. This framing prevented the liberal moniker. If swing voters did not think of us as parroting the national Democratic line, we could win independents unsure about Wilder on more conventional issues.

We had one path to victory from the moment Coleman beat Trible: turn him into an extremist on abortion. For weeks, our TV ads had quoted his extremist lines from earlier in the campaign. When Coleman tried to move back from the limb and suggest that the anti-abortion laws he promised would never get passed or that he was not going to be their staunchest advocate, we pretended those comments did not exist. When reporters would bring up the latest Coleman abortion wiggle, we did not care.

When the press called me, I would say, in effect, the quote attributed to Coleman in the ads is accurate. If he says this is no longer his position, why should we believe him? Moreover, it is not my job to parse through everything Marshall Coleman might say today, tomorrow, whenever. Coleman said it, we are going to remind voters that he said it and I do not give a damn whether he liked it, whether the press liked it, whether the *Times-Dispatch* called us whatever name it had yet to call us. If Coleman thinks we are misstating his position, he can call a press conference, he can run a TV ad calling us liars, it is up to him, that is his choice.

Greer and I had our differences about how to end the campaign. He wanted to take the high road and close with an uplifting message. He had produced a beautiful commercial of Wilder working amid the foliage and grass of a farm, talking about hopes and dreams. Greer called it "Rise Above," a phrase the narrator used. The words did not need further explanation, as the Coleman campaign now openly discussed its candidate being subjected to a "double standard." Greer felt we would benefit while Coleman sunk into the racial muck. For all my disagreements with Greer—and there were many—he was a very good person. He wanted to win the election not merely for credibility inside the consulting profession but because he was a liberal Democrat on social issues.

He made a passionate case for "Rise Above." If we won, it would be the ad of the decade, and Greer could claim this transcendent appeal won. If that could have been true, our staff would have been the first ones to create the Frank Greer award. But we were not going to overcome racism in that election by taking the high road. There was no high road to take or easy, nice way to sail over the muck. Greer's idealism had blinded him to reality: "Rise Above" meant losing.

Donilon and Petts had their numbers, which were still tilted to make the projections more Republican than the outcome. In that model, we were below 50 percent even counting all those leaning toward Wilder. The remaining undecided voters were all white.

Lafayette, the theologian, wanted to rip Coleman harder than anyone. If my memory is off here, I have to apologize, for Laura was and is a wonderful person.

Wilder had the final say and said no to "Rise Above." I agreed: we should kick Coleman through the finish. Our weekly polling showed we lost votes every time our abortion ad went off the air, so we kept it up right through Election Day.

The reason Coleman openly played the race card at the end is because he knew what we knew. If we did not have his extremist position on abortion, he wins. There were only two issues in the end: race and abortion. If it had been strictly race, we would have lost by 10 percent. There had been no way to rise above that but by the grace of the Supreme Court. Coleman's advisors had hoped we would let it go and assumed perhaps the abortion issue had played out by mid-October.

I remember Wilder telling me he had called Greer, who agreed not to "rise above" but rather go the "rise above my ass" low road that the rest of us agreed had to be done.

The Thursday before the election, I was home working on our Election Day game plan. I remember sitting at the desk working on an IBM clone a friend made for me. The Richmond media market loomed large in the campaign. The living room television played in the background so I could monitor the frequency of Coleman's ads. As I was working, I heard the transcendent orchestral from "Rise Above."

I started flipping channels. There were no cellphones back then. Wilder was out campaigning. Mike and Dave were out somewhere too, if I recall. I might have called Laura; I just cannot remember. I would have called Leslie if she were not at the apartment.

I nervously switched channels, not wanting to see what I knew I had heard. Then I saw "Rise Above" during the 11:00 p.m. news. "Rise above."

I picked up the phone. Then I threw it across the room, and it slammed into the wall, creating a huge gash in the plaster.

I got Wilder on the miraculously functioning phone. I wanted to drive to D.C. and wring Greer's neck. Wilder said there was not much we could do that night, and he would handle it in the morning. But there was still time for Greer to call the TV stations and change the advertisement rotation. He could take out the slots reserved for his masterpiece and insert one of our commercials slamming Coleman on abortion. Back then, you had to place your weekend and Monday ads by Friday morning. Once in rotation, the computer program could not be changed until Monday afternoon. We pulled it in time. If I had not caught "Rise Above," we would have been stuck with it through the final crucial hours. Fortunately, I have always been able to fall asleep, get up and not carry yesterday with me.

I have never understood why Greer defied Wilder at the end. There were many theories. The bottom line is Greer wanted us to win and wanted to be known as the guy whose ad did it, so I have always given him the benefit of the doubt.

Wilder prevailed in the closest gubernatorial race in state history. To this day, it is the only one that has required a recount.

Governor Wilder's inauguration. *Library of Virginia.*

My job was to figure out the campaign framework. We all had to get the implementation right. The ads, the press releases, the candidate on the stump and in the debate—there were many moving parts and a lot of talented people. But even then, we needed luck, and we needed Coleman's campaign to misplay the issue; there were so many factors out of our control.

It was a long time ago. We won. That is enough to remember, really. The story is what the story is.

History records it as the most significant state campaign on abortion rights.[11] It was the first in a conservative state to show that this issue could no longer be dismissed. Republican women were tired of their party not realizing that times were changing, and men had to stop thinking they had the right to dictate these personal decisions. Abortion had become the galvanizing issue of the women's movement after *Webster*. The Wilder victory showed the power of women's issues to those Democrats who had been in doubt.

The campaign helped make another history. President Obama said that witnessing the victory as a law student made him lift his sights to realize it was a new day in terms of what he could achieve.

Nobody could have predicted this when Wilder set out to run for lieutenant governor five years before.

7

THE RAINY DAY FUND
AND THE BEST-MANAGED
STATE GOVERNMENT

The journey from worst- to best-managed state started during the transition from Governor Baliles to Governor-elect Wilder.[12] The governor-elect and I had the traditional transition budget meeting with Baliles and his aides in the conference room next to the governor's office on the third floor of the capitol.

Baliles had promised not to raise taxes during his 1985 campaign and never thought they would get caught fudging the numbers. Baliles's aides and Senator Hunter Andrews, the powerful chairman of the Senate Finance Committee, had tried to pull a fast one on the people. I knew Baliles and his staff were mad at Wilder for opposing his tax increase for transportation and for my exposure of its miscalculations. Wilder's aide Joel Harris once told me the Baliles people had banned me from the Governor's Mansion after I helped expose their transportation plan's bait-and-switch. To be fair, Joel would say a lot of things that were not necessarily false but were not necessarily the gospel truth, either. He had a penchant for "stirring things up," I would say—and I would venture that he would agree this is a fair assessment or perhaps even too mild.

During the campaign, Baliles called me out of the blue one evening a day or so before his debate with Republican Wyatt Durrette. To this day, I do not know why he called—I mean, the real reason. Ostensibly, he wanted my opinion on taxes. He said the polls showed him vulnerable on only that issue. I knew this could hardly be a surprise. In the 1980s, Virginia Republicans essentially had only that one issue. The late-night

1985 phone call would be the only one of its sort between Baliles and me. Yet it was a phone call to remember.

The tax issue had worked against Howell in the 1977 gubernatorial election—but he had long been the GOP boogeyman. Chuck Robb helped Virginia turn the corner on that brand of politics. Ex-Marine Robb had a different image and spent his term as lieutenant governor telling every Virginian to know this about him: he wasn't a progressive, knee-jerk, pro-union, pro-women's rights, love-them-liberals type like the GOP said about the Norfolk populist. I get his politics of distancing himself from Howell. Governor Robb, elected in 1981, had not raised taxes. Even during the Reagan recession, Virginia state budget revenues went up.

Baliles faced Durrette in a rematch, of sorts. The conventional wisdom had predicted Durrette as the favorite to defeat Baliles for attorney general in 1981. However, on an analytical basis, this seemed based on one assumption. Durrette, then a delegate from Northern Virginia, would in theory run exceptionally strong there in an election in which Nova was also considered Robb country. There would be a sizable number of Robb-Durrette voters, the thinking went, sufficient to give the GOP candidate a win despite the top of the ticket losing. Robb did win Northern Virginia, and there were a lot of split-ticket voters. In the region's biggest jurisdiction, Fairfax County, Robb won by a narrow 4 percent margin while Durrette carried it by 16 percent. But the Democratic wave sweeping across the Commonwealth for Robb, along with the even larger margins for lieutenant governor candidate Dick Davis, pulled Baliles to a narrow twenty-six-thousand-vote win, 51–49 percent. This close loss convinced GOP convention delegates to pick Durrette as the candidate for governor. But 1985 would be another tough year for the GOP. When Baliles called me, his campaign seemed a sure winner over Durrette's floundering effort, due in part to dissension in GOP ranks.

Baliles came right to the point. He wanted my opinion on one thing: should he pledge not to raise taxes? I felt the same way back then as I do today: why did he want my opinion? He had highly capable managers like David Doak and Darryl Martin running his campaign. His press secretary, Chris Bridge, could play hardball with the best of them. He had other sharp politicos like Bill Wiley, Corey Roberts, Barry Rose and Larry Framme, to name a handful. David McCloud, then Robb's chief of staff and later Baliles's, understood politics.

I thought Baliles had answered his own question. He had made certain to avoid the "taxer" label for years in anticipation of a run for governor. Why change now? Unless, of course, he intended to propose raising taxes once safely in the governor's chair. Why call me and why now? Whatever the rationale, he did call, and he did ask my opinion.

I held the phone, looking around the room. Then it hit me: in the 1981 campaign, candidate Robb had never unequivocally said, "Read my lips, no new taxes," as George H.W. Bush would say when running for president. In the language of Virginia politics, the preferred mantra had long been simply to promise an administration committed to "fiscal responsibility." That is how Robb phrased his stance on taxes, to the applause of the Byrd editorial boards and business leaders.

Four years before, Republican gubernatorial candidate Marshall Coleman had taken the "no tax" pledge then growing in popularity among backers of President Reagan. But the business community was not diametrically opposed to any taxes, just taxes that weighed more heavily on them. They might want another gas tax, for example, but a rigid pledge nixed any such measure. Coleman had been panned by business conservatives for being irresponsible, the reason being that no one can predict the future and it might be necessary to raise taxes to maintain the state's AAA bonding, the gold standard of fiscal responsibility. Robb had wisely criticized Coleman's position as a good soundbite but not a true marker of a prudent, fiscally responsible candidate.

Baliles knew Robb would not push back should Baliles, his chosen successor, make a no tax pledge. But if he adopted the Robb posture from 1981, did he worry that Wilder would go further and take the no tax pledge? We had, in fact, taken that pledge, but it had not been part of the narrative of the lieutenant governor campaign. Moreover, Baliles knew it would not be in Wilder's interest to get crosswise with Robb on anything. Since I could not imagine Baliles thinking differently, I asked myself again: Why is he calling me?

My advice seemed obvious enough: you should do what you think is right. He understood. I gained nothing, nor did Wilder, by telling him to lie. Baliles was no fool: he could play politics skillfully. If he intended not to raise taxes, then there was no reason for the call. Therefore, I knew that he intended to raise taxes after he was elected. I figured they would be for education. He and Robb believed in education. It had changed Baliles's life.

HIGHWAY BUILDING AND ROAD maintenance were funded on a user fee basis, which is how Harry Byrd made the reputation that put him in the

Democratic Party driver's seat for forty years. In the 1920s, the business-political establishment wanted to issue bonds to pay for new roads. Byrd guessed the state's dominant rural voters wanted roads but not government debt. So he proposed raising the gas tax, which was immortalized in his future "pay as you go" mantra: raise cash to build roads, and do not allow politicians to get the state hooked on debt financing.

I had not thought about that 1985 call when Wilder and I arrived on the third floor of the capitol for the transition budget briefing. Wilder had me along for one major reason: I had a Baliles B.S. detector (or so I believed). The detector proved handy. There is no other way to say it: the Baliles crew flat-out lied to Wilder with Baliles in the room. They would later claim they were thunderstruck when discovering, sometime after the meeting, that state budget revenues suddenly dropped off the proverbial fiscal cliff in the later weeks of December 1989, leaving Wilder the worst deficit of any state.

I can still see Baliles's budget maven standing there spinning his fiscal fairy tale. Paul Timmreck made a career in top government and public university finance jobs. He knew numbers. He had produced a budget to Baliles's specifications and filled it with all the governor's promises. He said it might be expensive, but the state could pay for all the teacher raises and other politically attractive ornaments aimed at making his boss exceedingly popular as he left office. He sold it far better than Donald Trump.

I did not buy it. I do not have Wilder's poker face. I thought, "Surely he isn't believing this fiscal fantasy. It sounds too good to be true." Moreover, Baliles did have a new, unexpected issue to raise. He wanted to do something with a state property in Virginia Beach. I recall him laying a map on the conference room table and discussing his proposal. It seemed to make a lot of sense. But why do it at this meeting? That seemed odd.

As we left the meeting and began heading over to the transition office, he asked, "What did you think?"

I knew he was not asking a question. He already knew what I suspected.

"They ain't telling us something—and that Virginia Beach thing, what the hell was that?" I said, or words to that effect.

He gave me a look and a smile. He also smelled a rat. There was no need to have a big discussion.

The transition budget briefing had been given, as traditionally required. But the true state of the Commonwealth's budget would only be known, at least to the governor-elect, when he got the key to the Governor's Office.

A FEW WEEKS LATER, I found out at Wilder's first cabinet meeting. It was in the same conference room as the transition briefing. The same Paul Timmreck gave a budget presentation—but this time, he was the secretary of finance, the boss of the budget director.

I had not wanted Timmreck as secretary of finance. The governor had also created a new deputy chief of staff role for Bob Schultz, a brilliant budget guy picked from the General Assembly staff. I would soon nickname them "T and S" for Tax and Spend, sometimes to their faces. As the adage goes, humor is the most serious form of communication. They were far better numbers guys than I. On the other hand, so what? Being numbers smart is not enough. The truth is, at that level, fiscal policy has defining political dimensions.

They now said Virginia faced its biggest budget deficit in history and the largest gap on a percentage basis of any state in the country. Our 10 percent shortfall was bigger than it was during the Great Depression. They wanted Wilder to break his no tax pledge.

"Why didn't you tell the governor these numbers last month?" I asked Timmreck.

"I didn't work for him back then," came the answer without hesitation.

I thought it cowardly and disqualifying. I still do. Wilder's role as incoming governor required proposing amendments to the two-year budget submitted by the outgoing chief. But Wilder accepted Timmreck's explanation.

Some say after that I always had it out for Timmreck, but that is not right. I felt that Wilder was the boss and that if he could live with Timmreck, so could I. That did not mean I had to agree with his advice. My issue with Timmreck, Schultz, Senator Andrews and Delegate Dickie Cranwell—the brains of the House of Delegates, in my view, a man who might have been governor—was simple: they wanted Wilder to break his no tax pledge and do a Baliles 2.0 as soon as possible.

I asked Timmreck when our economists said the recessionary drop in revenues was likely to end. The state has a board of economic wizards appointed to prevent a governor from being caught unawares by economic events. They are brilliant. They know their stuff—until they do not.

"It will stabilize soon," was the answer.

I proposed taking money from the new state lottery and putting it into the general fund. Baliles had wanted the money used to fund new building construction and said other funds should be dedicated to education. I feared earmarking it for education would lead to what happens in other states: the legislature would simply reduce what they had previously decided to give to the education budget by the same amount. There would be no education funding increase, only an illusion.

Wilder opted to put the lottery money in the general fund. He wanted it used for education and safety net services the state provided to those in need. He also made it clear that there would be no tax increase. We are going to once and for all find out where all the unnecessary spending exists, he said, then cut it out. When the smoke clears, we will be lean and efficient, at which point a discussion of new revenues might make sense.

In truth, any budget can be balanced if all one has to do is match inflow and outflow. It is a math problem and there are any number of gimmicks. Sleights of hand will catch up eventually, but a clever governor can avoid the day of reckoning for several years, at least.

Wilder wanted to finally do a real budget review. To his credit, Timmreck did it. Was it his first choice? I doubt it, but he did a good job. I respected him for that, even if we did not see eye to eye.

<hr />

WILDER ALSO WANTED LEVERAGE over Senator Andrews, the best deal man in the General Assembly. They had served together in the Senate. Andrews might be overbearing, but the man was a budget magician. The Tidewater lawman knew the numbers better than any governor, so he always managed to get the best deal. Challenging the Senate finance chair had never worked.

While jogging one day, I thought of a way to outfox the General Assembly, outgame Andrews and, most importantly, put Wilder on the national map as the best financial manager of any state in the nation. Additionally, it would be exceptionally good for the future of education and the state's finances. Win-win-win really. It was an elegant play that I figured Andrews would admire after realizing he had been checkmated.

No governor in the country intentionally ran a surplus during a recession. It made no sense on the surface. During flush times, a few states required their governors to stock away cash for the next downturn; Utah was the exemplar. No state took some of the revenue out and purposely refused to spend it during a recession. Why cut more and make people less happy? The proverbial rainy day had arrived.

My reading of political history indicated this truism: it was better to cut too much than too little when facing a budget crunch. This seemed particularly true when the incoming governor inherited a problem from the outgoing one. The early painful cuts can be blamed on the previous occupant, but if you must keep cutting, that is on you.

Wilder inherited a budget meltdown that Baliles had hidden from him and the public. It mattered not in the final analysis. The public would expect the new governor to fix the mess irrespective of the cause.

"Governor," I said, "you should not merely balance the budget but run a planned surplus." The reasons seemed plain enough, I argued to Wilder over dinner at the Governor's Mansion. We would eat on the second floor of the residence, in a smallish room in the living quarters. Everyone enjoyed being invited to dinner at the Mansion due to the lavish food. I would usually order a baked potato, sliced tomatoes and orange juice. I like to eat what I like to eat. I have since learned that white potatoes are not good for you and switched to sweet.

My pitch went this way. First, the blue-chip economists advising the state could not guarantee stabilization anytime soon. This meant revenues would likely keep falling and there would be more cuts in the future. Therefore, forcing bigger cuts in nonessential services right now and setting those savings aside in a reserve fund controlled by the governor made good policy and political sense. Timmreck, Andrews and the House of Delegates finance leaders would point out this required making more cuts than would be needed to balance the budget. That might be true in the future, I conceded, but they also had items they could cut. Putting aside $200–$300 million in a rainy day fund would be heralded as sound fiscal management. That some of this praise might come from national newspapers and magazines seldom fans of Democrats like Wilder should not dissuade us. Moreover, we could blame these cuts on the inherited recession and the debunked Baliles projections.

Secondly, if you want to be a top fiscal manager, you cannot come back every year and say, sorry, but I have to cut more. Unless you are seen as having done all you possibly can and that no one could have been reasonably expected to do more. Here again, it made good policy and political sense to have a stash of cash for an even rainier day.

Thirdly, I pointed out to Wilder his complaint about lacking leverage with Andrews in the Senate and the Democratic leadership in the House of Delegates. Money talks, I said: if you ask for $200–$300 million to put in a rainy day fund and say you won't sign a budget unless it has one, they will have to do it. You have leverage if you make clear that you alone decide when this reserve fund gets to be distributed into the general fund.

The proposal seemed a no-brainer. Raising taxes in the first year would win support in the General Assembly; on the editorial pages of the *Washington*

Post, *Virginian-Pilot* and *Roanoke Times*; and among various special interests. But the average Virginian, especially those who took a leap of faith to back Wilder, would feel double-crossed, far more than they did when Baliles broke his no tax pledge. America's other governors balance their budgets and hope the bleeding stops. Only Wilder would go further, hedge against more bad times and run a big surplus. I wanted Wilder to get his chance to be the governor he wanted to be.

Wilder had already gone on television to address the state and laid out his plans to cut back on programs we could defer to fund services Virginians needed to have. "Necessities, not niceties," he said, a resonant line from Laura Lafayette, I believe. Implementation would be tough. The General Assembly would try to avoid funding cuts affecting special interests, and Wilder would need to ensure Timmreck protected the safety net and education. Timmreck did a terrific job.

Wilder needed to get a handle on state finances. He knew the Democrats controlling the General Assembly always felt in charge. Wilder smartly tried to get Republicans, although a small minority, to help. For the first time in state history, so far as I could recall, a Democratic governor invited the GOP delegation to talk finances at the Mansion.

My goal in advising Wilder to be a stickler for fiscal responsibility centered on trying to change a corrupted system where the powerful used every crisis to further economic inequity. What taxes did Andrews and other politicians want to raise? There was only one: the sales tax, a regressive tax. It might have been possible to justify such a measure, I thought, depending on the use of the new revenues. But they raised the sales tax during the Baliles administration to build roads, not schools. Roads were supposed to be built with user fees, not working mothers when they bought diapers, clothing and books for their children. Road builders had too much sway. Since 1989, the General Assembly has raised the sales tax three more times, four if you count the local option sales tax. Did it dedicate the proceeds primarily to education even once? No—only the segregationist governor and General Assembly did that, fifty-five years ago.

Wilder got his rainy day surplus as a line item in the budget.

National media, led by the *Wall Street Journal*, took notice. Doug Wilder, history maker, had done the unimaginable: kept his campaign promise not to raise taxes. He funded the safety net but not the usual special interest goodies. Writers and commentators on national politics began speculating about Wilder's future. The first elected Black American governor, a progressive on social policy, was turning out to be a tough budget cutter. During the campaign, I had called it the New Mainstream: social progressivism tied to common sense fiscal moderation.

It seemed to surprise the northeastern media. They had a picture of Wilder as a southern Black man fighting reactionaries. They believed Wilder was a liberal, or more to the point, they thought the "right" Black politician would be a tax-and-spend liberal, not a budget hawk.

UNFORTUNATELY, THE RECESSION KEPT grinding on, lowering revenues even further. There came a time when Wilder had to put the finishing touches on another budget. I got a call from Jay Shropshire, chief of staff, saying Wilder wanted to see me that night.

The call came not long before sunset. I was at home with Leslie. Normally, Wilder and I would just talk over the phone. "Something is up, don't you think?" she said. She made sure my hair looked good, and I had my tie on right. We were living in Short Pump, roughly thirty minutes by car to the statehouse in the days when that area was mostly farmland. I remember the Capitol Police letting me park near the Governor's Mansion. I likely ran up the capitol stairs instead of waiting for the slow elevator.

In 1989, the governor's office likely ranked among the smallest in the nation, if not the smallest. A living room in a decent apartment had more space. Shropshire's office had a couple of chairs, a desk, a few bookshelves and one window. It was the least impressive office on the third floor, but it sat outside of the most important door in the building.

"What's up?" I said.

Shropshire had his usual big smile and country charm. He was impossible not to like. "What's up, Goldilocks?" he said. I was always "Goldilocks" to Jay; he would say it with a huge grin.

Normally, the governor had me go right into his office. That night, I sat in the chair across from Shropshire's desk for at least twenty minutes. It was unusual; I cannot recall a similar situation.

Usually, Shropshire would be on the phone, chain-smoking while cajoling some legislator or lobbyist. His desk lacked the document stacks surely found on those of the forty-nine other chiefs around the country. He reveled in the politics of the job, not the policy: he had been the longtime clerk of the Senate, which is how he first met Wilder. That night, he sat at his desk reading the *Richmond Times-Dispatch*.

Suddenly, the governor opened the door to his inner sanctum.

"Mr. Chairman," he said.

Some people called me that, but few used it in a friendly fashion except for Wilder. I found it funny; I certainly did not feel like a chairman. No one in the Democratic Party leadership wanted me to be party chair except Wilder. He needed an ally he could trust. He knew I would be willing to draw fire from officials who never wanted him to be lieutenant governor, much less the state's chief executive.

"How's Leslie?" Wilder asked.

He never quite said it, but I think he was somewhat amazed that a sensible, attractive, fashionable woman like her would hang with me. That made two of us: we were something of an odd couple. He was putting on the charm.

"She's good."

He likely thought I had deduced the reason for the late summons. Actually, I had not the foggiest clue.

"I just got off the phone with Timmreck," he said.

As usual, he had told the governor there remained no excess spending to cut. Maybe a nip here, a tuck there, a couple of million in total, tops. But after that? He and his team had done all they could without starting to cut into the bone of state government.

It was time for a tax increase or at least the release of the rainy day fund. Andrews and the rest would be on the same page. By now, even Wilder's detractors were saying he did a great job saving the safety net, which meant that Timmreck did a great job and never got much credit. The same could be said for others on his staff and in the Governor's Office who worked 24/7.

Wilder launched into a monologue about the budget. Timmreck had said enough is enough, Andrews had pressed and pressed, as had the House folks. Wilder said I had no idea how much pressure they were putting on him.

By now, I realized Leslie's instincts had been right: the governor had called me down to explain why he had released the rainy day money—the planned surplus, the national maneuvering money, his stack of chips in the game—for Timmreck to use in drafting the new budget proposals. The old guard wanted a new tax—but for now, the rainy day fund would do.

I remember Wilder standing behind his desk looking at me seated ten feet away. At that moment, I could tell being governor had ceased to be fun. The recession had taken a toll on his popularity, as it had executives across the country. National politicians have the option of deficit spending.

"You were right to recommend the surplus," Wilder said. "People see that now." Good psychology. "It's done its job," he added.

Timmreck had won the fight for the surplus. So had Andrews, Dickie Cranwell and the others. The rainy day fund had become associated with me. I figured Shropshire already knew, as did others on staff. I understood where Timmreck and the others were coming from. But Timmreck, in my view, had been outfoxed by Andrews.

I told Wilder the truth, as I have always tried to do.

"Governor, with all due respect, I think there is a better play here," I said. He asked me to explain.

I started off by saying I understood why he had to put the surplus into the pot. I thought it was a good move. I did not say this to flatter him; I never did that. The fiscal rain kept falling, so that is when you are supposed to use your rainy day.

My problem rested with the timing. In my view, Timmreck had forced Wilder to give up his leverage for nothing.

"It is your money, not Andrews's," I said.

Right now, he controlled a fund that no one could touch politically. We knew that ultimately it would need to be not just a budget item but a constitutional amendment establishing a fund tappable only by order of the governor, and then only under certain conditions. Establishing a rainy day fund in the constitution would guarantee Wilder's place as the nation's top fiscal manager. But constitutional amendments took time, so right now it was a match between Wilder and the General Assembly.

Timmreck had been played by Andrews. Yes, the governor technically had to be the first to spend the rainy day money, in this case, to fund the governor's priorities. But, as I pointed out, once the surplus money got allocated in the Governor's budget proposal, it would then be available for Andrews and the General Assembly to move around as they saw fit through its own budget process. After the budget passed the legislature, that left Wilder with only the veto pen.

Timmreck was a numbers guy, not a politician. Wilder did not think Timmreck had been played, but he did realize if Timmreck had talked to me, I could have made him the hero in the saga. The governor told me to sit quietly. He dialed Timmreck himself.

"I think we will need to keep the rainy day fund for now," he told Timmreck. "We need to redo the budget."

I can still hear Timmreck shouting into the phone as Wilder held it smiling at arm's length.

The budget was due to be printed shortly. A change this late would require great effort, and I figured he had already assured Andrews and the others he had the problem under control.

"It's Goldman, isn't it?" Timmreck said.

Wilder said no. And he was right: I merely set the chess board. Wilder saw how his secretary of finance had missed the move. Wilder did not blame Timmreck, and neither did I. As I said, he was a money guy, not a political guy.

I left the Governor's Office, gave Shropshire a thumbs up, exited through the side door and went home. I do not recall talking with Wilder or Timmreck about the budget again.

I gave the governor my best advice. I made and remade my case for what I felt he needed to do, both in the moment and for a permanent rainy day fund. I knew he could get it done.

———

IN 1992, THE GENERAL Assembly put a constitutional amendment to create the Revenue Stabilization Fund to the requisite vote of the people. It passed with 72.6 percent. The rainy day fund changed fiscal management and instituted new budget discipline in the Commonwealth. No longer would the legislature spend whatever came in. It was forced to save unexpected revenues in flush times, which prevented wasting precious education dollars and safety net money on other projects. The fund grew to over $1 billion in relatively short order. When hard times came, funds would be available to support education and other safety net services.

Without Wilder, it never would have happened. A rainy day fund is the opposite of what the Virginia political class wanted. They preferred to spend surpluses, not save them, and then, when things got tough, they would raise regressive taxes and preserve special interest spending. Governors since Wilder always have had a backup when dealing with budget shortfalls. Over the past thirty years, the rainy day fund has therefore saved many billions of dollars for education and working class and poor Virginians.

Ideally, such fiscal innovation should come from lawmakers eager to save the public's money. But Wilder found no partners, at least in the beginning. To be fair, Timmreck always supported the creation of such a fund, as did the others. They realized it was long overdue. It would eventually be considered among Wilder's most lasting achievements.

8

AN OUTSIDER BECOMES PARTY CHAIR

A Free White Man Confronts the Virginia Way Mindset

I t took twenty-nine years before I finally realized why my being white, Jewish and northern so upset the establishment.

In 2006, I was invited to meet some of the most prominent Jewish leaders in central Virginia. They were good people, pillars of the community. I had never been asked to discuss my politics with any of them in a forum, much less individually, and I looked forward to a useful, open discussion. Surprisingly, the attendees had apparently been waiting twenty-nine years to get something off their collective chests.

Henry Howell had been the first Democrat to openly fight the anti-Semitic Byrd Machine and be nominated for governor. Jewish business leaders in Tidewater had been his biggest private backers. Richmond businessman Sidney Lewis, known to all men at the meeting, gave Howell the largest contribution in state history at the time, $300,000. Howell's opponent, Mills Godwin, the last Byrd Machine governor, ensured voters knew Lewis's religion. Godwin blamed aides for campaign materials pointing out that Lewis went to temple. The attendees knew all about that.

I was not a stranger to the people at the meeting, at least in terms of knowing what I had done over the years. They knew about my being Wilder's chief cook and bottle washer, my years as party chair and my successful efforts heading the referendum drive reforming Richmond government in 2003. I figured they wanted to get to know me. My name had been in the paper as a possible candidate for city council in Richmond's First District, its most conservative and my home. I had not previously considered running for any office and knew I could not win a head-to-head race against anyone aligned with the GOP in the district. But there seemed likely to be a five-way contest. If all five stayed as active candidates to the end, the electoral math indicated a pathway to victory with perhaps 35 percent or so of the vote.

Over the years, I have been dubbed the "miracle worker" for helping Wilder tear down the "Whites Only" sign from the door leading to statewide office in the South, then the "No Blacks Need Apply" sign from the door on governors' offices across America.[13] There have been fewer flattering descriptions of my politics. Wilder often said in speeches that if you become infatuated with flattery, then criticism will crush you. I had learned to accept the good with the bad, the praise with the pummeling.

I had never been called a pushy Jew before so directly in state politics. They did not, of course, use the term; rather, they merely said my politics were embarrassing to them, that Jews were not supposed to be assertive in Virginia politics, they were supposed to do things behind the scenes, that I was too loud, too liberal… "That is not how we do things here" sums it up. Two of the participants used words to that effect, though I do not recall the others speaking much, if at all.

I remember thinking: it is a good thing my father is not alive. While in World War II, there were a couple of southern boys who kept riding him, using the J-word. They were far bigger than he. There came a time when he refused to let them keep saying it. One afternoon, they started up in a crowded locker room. He went up the biggest one, a mountain of man, and said they should settle the matter outside. Everyone in the room knew the southern boy would crush him. They tried to restrain my father, but he would not listen. Suddenly, the big southern boy said he was sorry. He had not really meant any harm or offense.

"I just never met any Jew before," my dad recalled him saying. "I just was repeating what I learned back home."

"Truth is," my dad responded, "I never met anyone from your parts, either. So maybe I was reacting the same way."

All shook hands. They became best friends, as my dad told the story. They would go out drinking and helped beat Hitler together. "Those guys likely saved my life," he said.

His way of dealing with the situation was not mine. I had no intention of trying to make friends with people who treated me like Ralph Ellison's *Invisible Man*. This meeting occurred more than three generations later, but they could not see Paul Goldman. They saw only what they wanted.

I asked myself, Why did they want to meet me? They already had their minds made up. I have attended any number of similar meetings over the years but few, if any, like this one. They had no intention of backing me if I ran for office.

I smiled and listened to them beat down my character and my politics, never suggesting in the least that I had done anything useful. I can still remember keeping a frozen, polite smile. I remember thinking: *Who the hell did they think there were?* At the end of the meeting, the leader said they wanted me to know the reasons they could not back me if I ran for council and the reasons they did not think someone like me should be in public office. I did not respond, merely nodded, thanked everyone and walked out the door.

Over the next few days, my mind examined the meeting from various angles. I realized there was an important lesson here, something I had never previously appreciated over my years in politics. Slowly, a long-overlooked truth began dawning on me.

These Richmonders were good men. They were at the top of the food chain and would surely be called enlightened. Yet their words seemed but a paraphrase of those southern boys my father had set straight more than sixty years earlier. The boys my father ran into were uneducated and raised in a hardscrabble existence, yet when confronted with what they thought they knew, they realized they did not really know anything about my father or his beliefs. When faced with their ignorance, they were smart enough to realize it and change. They had enough respect for themselves and gave it to a fellow soldier. They might need each other to save their lives.

The men in the meeting were among the most privileged in Virginia. These were intelligent, good, charitable men who supported worthy causes. They had either been raised in a segregated society or had come to it early and stayed to make their fortunes. They knew the Byrd Machine's bigotry extended to anti-Semitism.

They were by no means required to like me—indeed, they may have considered Howell and Wilder anti-business, too liberal and so forth. I remember talking to Leslie about it. We were separated by this time. In some ways, I think we better understood each other compared to when we were married. Thomas stayed mostly with me, as he was attending Mary Munford School. Perhaps I knew what she was going to say and wanted to hear it. She did not seem surprised—quite the opposite. What the hell did you expect? is the look I remember.

My northern brain had missed the meaning of Chief Justice Earl Warren's opinion in *Brown v. Board*. Virginia had been a defendant in the case. Warren justified his decision in part by saying the segregation of the races in public education led to a "sense of inferiority" among minority students since "separating the races is usually interpreted as denoting the inferiority of the negro group."

I must have read those words fifty times over the years. Every time, I read them solely as discussing how segregation made Black Americans feel inferior. But now I realized I missed the message Chief Justice Warren had sent the white population, one far too radical to be spoken aloud by him back in 1954. His conclusion was so obvious yet so taboo: if segregation gave Black students a false sense of inferiority, then it logically instilled in white students a false sense of superiority. The segregationists understood this would be a subtle, unappreciated implantation of a value critical to their caste system. The white students would not appreciate this unspoken manipulation by those fostering segregated education. I had never properly understood the other side of the coin and its equally damaging psychological impact. Without even realizing it, the most progressive white minds in Virginia had been seeded with a feeling of superiority not based in fact or achievement.

This indoctrination was not limited to white supremacy. There were whites and then there were favored whites. Think of the eugenics movement in Virginia. In 1924, the General Assembly passed both the Racial Integrity Act outlawing interracial marriage and the Virginia Sterilization Act legalizing eugenics. The bulk of the known victims are white, and the biggest category in this general group are poor white rural women. The white elite that controlled state government saw them as being inferior white people.

As noted in chapter 5, the 1902 Constitution establishing segregation as the supreme law of Virginia took the limited voting rights away from nine-tenths of Black and half of all white citizens then allowed to vote.[14] The minority population, even if it had been allowed to vote, could not decide a statewide election. But the disenfranchised white vote could swing an election if put back on the rolls. Segregation in Virginia had always been more about creating a controlled white vote. The numbers were obvious. This is the reason the proposed 1902 white supremacy constitution had not been put to a statewide referendum, as new Virginia constitutions ordinarily were; the powerbrokers rammed through the new constitution by a mere act of the General Assembly.

I viewed segregation through the eyes of an oppressed religious minority, so I had not fully appreciated the need to see segregation as a means to impose a caste system on the white majority population. Segregation required two types of white supremacy. The white supremacist mindset demarcated generation after generation: white elite/middle class over white poor, and white poor over racial minorities.

Howell understood the dual facets of white supremacy. The champion of long-oppressed minority communities struck fear into the hearts of the establishment due to his ability to draw Black votes, but that alone would not be enough to win a gubernatorial primary. Their fear of Howell stemmed from the Norfolk populist's ability to challenge the foundation of the white caste system that segregation had instilled in the population's minds. Howell understood the poll tax could be overturned as an unconstitutional device to disenfranchise Black Virginians. At the same time, toppling it meant disenfranchised whites who understood elite whites saw them as inferior could vote.

In my view, this is what Professor Sabato meant by saying that Howell lost his race for governor because those hosting cocktail parties would never have invited him, if I may paraphrase. Howell might have been highly educated; he might have been a great lawyer; he might have a terrific sense of humor. But Henry and Betty Howell were not the neighbors you invited to parties. Indeed, they did not even live in that kind of neighborhood. Howell was not their kind of white person: he had thick glasses, and his politics were focused on the white working class— the rednecks, in their mind.

When running as a segregationist in 1965, Mills Godwin had lost Fairfax County and had lost Arlington by 8 percent. In 1973, Mills Godwin carried Fairfax County by 5 percent and barely lost Arlington County. There are numerous variables in all elections, but he did worse running as a known bigot than he did running against the state's greatest reformer eight years later.

Segregation's dual mindset of superiority had taken a terrible toll on the elite whites who led the Democratic Party. They believed that the elite white person in Virginia should act a certain way and imbue their beliefs with the attitude of what Senator Mark Warner refers to as the "Virginia Way."[15] They had decided to constrain themselves within the system to achieve their other goals. It is a legacy of segregation.

Howell was seen by elite whites as challenging the Virginia Way. It was partly due to his appearance, unavoidable in the electronic media age. When Howell was rising through the ranks, a candidate could pose for a picture and have all the details in place before the camera snapped the shot. Television changed the imagery of politics. His first commercials back in the 1960s were planned to shock and to be memorable, given his lack of money. Howell is not recognized today as a genius in terms of understanding the messaging of the new medium, but he grasped how it worked before any other major politician. Ironically, his knowledge proved a double-edged sword. He knew how to become memorable on only a shoestring budget. Thus, he got his first message across before the Byrd Machine could have suspected it. That first impression was the lasting one: he had exposed the old guard, loudly, with thick glasses and a tinny voice. Howell's politics had been right, but his image wrong. Godwin's politics were abhorrent, but his image was gubernatorial. Godwin had the cultured air of someone who seemed like a fine man to invite to a cocktail party.

Dr. King criticized the "white moderate" in "Letter from Birmingham Jail." Whatever Howell's virtues, many white Democrats who might be sympathetic to his politics felt he was attacking them for acquiescing to segregation because they knew they could benefit from it. They took his tone, his appearance and his challenges to the party personally, not politically. Segregation had forced many whites to make accommodations. Everyone had dreams, and nearly all are good people in their own minds. They *were* good people. Howell had not made such accommodations, yet here he was, close to being governor. That defied the Virginia Way.

In my northern mind, Howell was a courageous progressive figure challenging Black oppression. I had badly overestimated the importance of segregationist policies and underestimated the value of deeply ingrained personal identities. I had no idea white identity, especially the white identity of Democratic elite leadership, would feel so threatened.

In Virginia, every politician was Black or white first and foremost. I never understood it.

Richard Nixon and his campaign strategists understood. In 1968, Nixon carried Virginia with 43.4 percent. Segregationist George Wallace got 23.5 percent, and Democrat Hubert Humphrey received only 32.5 percent. The first test of Nixon's infamous Southern Strategy that would remake the Republican Party and produce his 1972 landslide started with the 1969 Virginia gubernatorial race. Nixon believed he could bring the Wallace white conservative vote into his Republican base. Republican Linwood Holton won 52.5 percent of the vote in 1969, compared to his bare 37.7 percent in 1965. In that contest, the Virginia version of George Wallace, William Story, ran on the Conservative Party ticket and got 13.4 percent. Thus, the 1969 vote for Holton roughly equaled his 1965 total coupled with the reactionary Conservative Party vote. In 1972, Nixon carried Virginia with 68 percent of the popular vote, roughly equal to his and Wallace's combined 1968 total. Nixon won Virginia and swept the South. Carter took back the Oval Office in 1976 because he flipped every southern state that had gone for Nixon—except Virginia.

Howell tried to do what Colonel Miller had done: slay the segregationists and white supremacy directly. Howell simply did not understand the white superiority of so many Virginians; it was a Virginia Way white supremacy that would never embrace working-class views.

Soon Wilder came, and elite whites in the party also thought he was on a fool's mission. They identified with Sabato, who believed that only a white person could win statewide. After Wilder won the governorship and defeated the segregationist mantra of white superiority, I mistakenly thought that the old "Virginia Way" mindset would be gone, at least in Democratic Party politics. I was wrong.

⎯⎯⎯⎯

THE 2006 MEETING SHOWED me what I did not appreciate in 1990 when Wilder appointed me to be chair of the state party. Had I known what is clear now, I would never have taken the job.

I knew I was politically inconvenient. The white Democratic Party elite did not want Wilder, but he had won. Over 1.5 million Virginians had voted for him in two different elections. He had earned it. To these same people, I had not earned it—indeed, quite the opposite: I had disqualified myself by challenging the establishment for twelve years straight.

The substantive case against me came down to this: I supposedly could not get along with anyone. I might have thought they sincerely believed it except for a most troublesome reality: the prior occupant was Larry Framme, Governor Baliles's choice. As a matter of law, the choice of party chair remains the sole authority of the Virginia Democratic Party Central Committee, but as a matter of politics, party activists cannot refuse a governor. I liked Framme and supported his nomination, as did Wilder. I remembered one editorial having praised his appointment as most worthy and appropriate given his ability to work with everyone. The proof they offered was his leadership in putting together the historic Baliles-Wilder coalition.

This referred to what the state's political commentators called the remarkable emergence of a coalition between two candidates. Pundits pegged Attorney General Baliles the underdog conservative, and Senator Wilder had been called the most liberal candidate to ever run for any party nomination by the Republicans. Baliles's biggest supporters were terrified by the prospect of him running on the same ticket as Wilder. If Wilder had any hope of cutting a deal, commentators opined that it would be with the liberal running for the Democratic gubernatorial nomination, Lieutenant Governor Dick Davis. Given that narrative, the unexpected announcement of the Baliles-Wilder coalition shocked the political elite. When both men went on to win not only nomination but also election, Framme seemed a genius as the official head of the Baliles-Wilder coalition. Both winners lived in the Third Congressional District, where Larry chaired the party's Third District Committee.

On paper, Larry did seem like the guy who had done the impossible as the mastermind of the most unique coalitions in state history. He could therefore get along with anyone, said the newspapers. There was only one flaw: it was not true.

Framme knew that he had nothing whatsoever to do with finalizing the Baliles-Wilder coalition cutting a deal on convention delegates. If I can be blunt, I handled the Wilder side and never spoke to Framme; the campaigns agreed to have him as the titular head. When I called him to discuss press tactics, he had a reaction a campaign manager does not forget: he first had to check with the Baliles campaign to make certain I was telling him the truth. The double standard as relates to both of our positions as party chairs requires pointing out.

Still, the establishment was right: I was not in the mold of any previous or, as it turns out, future party chair. Wilder figured he needed a party chair he could trust to have his back. The establishment knew I would back Wilder over them. I remain the only sitting chair to call on Democrats controlling the General Assembly to enact campaign finance and ethics reform. At my suggestion, the governor created a commission to make recommendations in this area. Twenty-nine years later, those recommendations are still too progressive for the Democrats running the General Assembly. I was the first chairman to point out the need to consider raising taxes to support education. I committed the party to helping fund elementary school education expenses for two young Virginians, one in the rural southwest, the other in an Eastern Virginia urban community. The policy caused a great deal of blowback. I was also no fan of President Clinton, whom I felt used minorities for political purposes to appear tough on crime.

These and other alleged trespasses of mine inevitably led to someone trying to have me removed as chair, the only time such a move has been done in party history. Senator Sonny Stallings from Virginia Beach took the lead, claiming total support from the General Assembly and party leadership.

The most important trespass involved 1990 redistricting.

The Democrats in the State Senate initially wanted redistricting to create two majority-minority districts. Wilder knew he could not agree to such a travesty of justice. I thought the law required creation of five, while the ACLU said the law required six. Wilder did the right thing, and I backed him. I also remember trying to create a Democratic district for Senator Jack Kennedy in the far southwest. He had just narrowly won a special election to the seat, and it would have been a rural white district. I had ordered the latest redistricting software and showed them how we could get him a Senate seat he could win without jeopardizing the other Democrats in that part of the state, but his Democratic Senate colleagues refused to do it. We sat there, using the computer at the party headquarters, as I showed them how to move the precincts. I kept trying, but they remained adamant. I liked Kennedy, but he must have rubbed some senior Democrats the wrong way.

Their biggest concern on that day turned out to be deciding who would tell Democratic Senate heavyweight Joe Gartlan that he would be losing a favorite precinct in redistricting. The senators in my office were actually afraid to tell him. They made clear their belief the Northern Virginia senator would blame the messenger. I remember reaching Gartlan on a cellphone. I delivered the bad news short and sweet, and he hung up.

Stallings lost reelection in 1991. He blamed Wilder and me for his and others' losses. He never directly blamed the creation of the five majority-minority districts, at least publicly. But he had a point: the creation of those five districts necessarily made other districts more Republican.

Senator Stallings had no reticence about going after me. His father had been a major political figure in the area, and Stallings rode his name into the Senate on plurality in 1987. This is commonplace in politics, of course. But the next election in 1991 drew 50 percent less voters. His district had been redrawn to include certain precincts containing military personnel who often failed to vote in nonpresidential election years. A number of candidates lost that year, and it was a good year for Republicans.

Stallings refused to accept any responsibility for his campaign. We had warned him about retribution from the National Rifle Association for introducing legislation they slammed as gun control. They were wrong, in my opinion, but they kept at it. I backed the bill. He was a Vietnam veteran and thumbed his nose publicly at the NRA. In the early 1990s, it took a brave, or foolhardy, Democrat to do that in a district a Republican could win. As I and others told Stallings: you only won with a plurality, a majority had voted against you. Take those NRA folks seriously; they do not play around.

A few months after his loss, Stallings's legislative friends began lobbying me to put him on a party committee. They said he needed something, and they would be grateful if I could do it for him. They knew I was not high on Stallings's Christmas card list. I knew he was close to Tom Moss and Ken Geroe, one my fiercest critics in the party, who had been an aide to Pickett and was angling to be chair.

I talked to Wilder's chief of staff, Jay Shropshire. He knew the coup would come at the upcoming June 1992 party convention, but, surprisingly, was for it. He would check around and later told me not to worry, Stallings would never act on his own. I decided to trust him and others.

Whatever the facts in the beginning, it did not take long before Stallings became the point man on an attempt to remove me as chairman at the upcoming state convention. My term ran until the middle of 1993, but I could be removed by a full vote of the convention. I forget the precise charges he leveled, but the gist of it was he claimed it was wrong for the party chair to be openly critical of Democrats.

I thought the charges were trumped up, but Sonny had a point: I was indeed critical of Democrats like Tom Moss. I did not see how Democrats could have as their Speaker an outspoken misogynist, an ERA opponent and someone who made racist remarks about the governor. I was no fan of Majority Leader Dickie Cranwell, the second-in-command in the House, but at least he was not a chauvinist. As Speaker, Moss would be chairman of the convention. Maybe Stallings, Geroe and Moss were in cahoots together, maybe not. I give Stallings credit where it is due. He saw his opportunity and took it.

I knew he had help from some people on the Wilder side. Stallings and his supporters did not know I knew. Pam Womack, then secretary of the Commonwealth, came to see me one day at the party office to warn me. Womack would not lie to me, and I pretended to be shocked. But—and I can reveal it now because it is years later—she surely had been used as a messenger. With no disrespect to Stallings—he served his country at war, so he is a much better fighter than me—he, too, was being used.

The truth is that if people had just asked and treated me with the respect I had earned, then I would have stepped down. Leslie and I had just been married, and the job did not then pay any money. They wanted my head on a pike to humiliate me.

I understood the game and could play it myself. My view remains the same: this crowd was prepared to be seen as racists during the campaigns and were prepared to stop Wilder solely because he was Black rather than suffering a historic defeat that would, in their minds, expose the state's racism. Wilder's win saved them from being labeled as racists, indeed saved the party from it.

Shropshire told me when they were going to make their move and asked me what I was going to do. I always kept Shropshire informed of my thinking and analysis. But I knew he was a double agent. He is smart. And he knew I knew.

The Steering Committee called a meeting where the top brass were supposed to confront me. I made sure Shropshire was sitting on my right. He brought the famed crime novelist and then-Richmond resident Patricia Cornwell to the meeting. I figured she might be scouting a venue for the case of the dead party chair. The party brass were trying to pressure me into resigning.

At the time, I thought it had to do with settling political scores. But as I say, after the 2006 meeting, I now understand it was deeper than that. I was not supposed to exist. I had not made any accommodation to the segregationist mindset. At a certain level, they saw my humiliation as proof of their righteousness. Wilder taught me that. They had the votes, but I had something better.

I knew statewide politics, but they saw only General Assembly politics. The public would see their knifing me as them knifing Wilder. He would have to defend me. They all wanted Attorney General Terry to be elected governor next year. How would humiliating me help her, especially when it would be seen by Democrats around the state as an attack on Wilder? At that instant, I realized Terry would never be governor even though she led by twenty-five points in the polls.

The white superiority instilled by the segregation regime had affected their judgment. Terry's people had never been comfortable with either Wilder or me. This happens all the time in politics, but if you study the smart players, they hold their nose and strive for unity. Historically, the play would have been to keep me on, or even give me a second term and leave me in the job until the election was over. You cut a deal and make an arrangement; that way the person most identified with Wilder in the public eye is on your side. This keeps Wilder and his constituency in your camp. Instead, Attorney General Terry stood by as they attempted their coup. When 1993 rolled around, she wanted me out instead of helping her campaign. The establishment thought they could not lose and were seeking retribution before Terry even got officially nominated.

Stallings and his crew tried, but my friends outsmarted them.

In early 1993, I suddenly resigned. It caught everyone by surprise, even Governor Wilder. Why did I do it? The reporters wrote stories full of silly analysis. If I served out my term and the Party Nominating Convention in June 1993 got to make the choice, the unwritten rule said Terry, as nominee, would get to pick the replacement. I figured Geroe or another anti-Wilder candidate would be her choice. I owed it to the governor to prevent that from happening.

I convinced Mark Warner to take the job—or maybe Mark already wanted it but pretended to be convinced. I knew Wilder would accept him as an interim appointment filling out the few months remaining in my term. The Steering Committee would technically pick my replacement, but I knew the Terry people would not dare dump Warner. I also knew he wanted to run for statewide office. This seemed to be a good way to lay the foundation for a future nomination. It was win-win-win. I got to block Geroe, preempt Terry and help Warner.

I owe a thank-you to the men at that 2006 meeting. That meeting crystallized what I felt for so long but had not recognized. I had my faults. But to them, the true fault was challenging the old Virginia mindset.

9

VMI'S EQUAL TREATMENT
OF WOMEN

Henry Howell is the best example of a statewide politician using the law to level the playing field and protect the rights of the average citizen. His first slogan, "Keep the Big Boys Honest," always stuck with me.

Virginia Military Institute was a symbol to Lost Cause glorifiers like Dominion Energy CEO Tom Farrell, whose depiction of Abraham Lincoln and others in *Field of Lost Shoes*—the revisionist Civil War film he wrote, paid for and acted in—is, to be polite, baffling for a guy of Farrell's intelligence. Similarly baffling was the hostility the old guard evinced to anyone who questioned certain things or who actually thought the Civil War amendments were as good as the original Bill of Rights. So many smart and educated Virginians seemed irrational in their views, but my northern mind simply did not realize how segregation had played with the heads of the state's leadership. VMI, like the Confederate flag, or cowardly Jefferson Davis who left in the middle of the night so women and children would face Grant's soldiers—why do these ignominious symbols and figures have such a grip on the minds of today's leading Virginians?

My lonely legal stance demanding that VMI accept women—as the U.S. Constitution firmly supported—made me a target of the boys' club in the General Assembly. In 1993, the establishment had bought into the deal made between VMI and nearby Mary Baldwin College, now Mary Baldwin University, to offer purportedly "separate but equal" military education at that historically women's college. VMI had an immensely powerful lobby, and the Fourth Circuit Court of Appeals had blinked under the pressure. My stance against that would not be upheld until 1996 by the Supreme Court in *U.S. v. Virginia*. Today, we remember Justice Ginsburg's historic decision.

In truth, the establishment network had been done with me long before VMI. Wilder's term had just ended. General Assembly Democrats watched their gubernatorial candidate, former attorney general Mary Sue Terry, lose after having a ten-to-twenty-point lead in every poll. The Democrats blamed Wilder for the loss. GOP legislators were feeling their oats, the party having won the Governor's Mansion for the first time since 1978. The winner, George Allen, came into office as the most partisan Republican chief executive in state history, then or since.

As the 1994 General Assembly session got going, the establishment could not wait to throw me off the State Council of Higher Education for Virginia (SCHEV), where I had made my position on VMI well known. Revenge? I actually never thought so. Revenge would require a feeling of personal betrayal. It was not revenge, nor was it illegal. Did they do it solely to kick Wilder as he left office? There had to be some of that. I know the game, so does Doug. As I recall, one of the ringleaders was Republican senator Bob Russell. I am not mad at him; he was trying to "make his bones" in the party, and I understood it was nothing personal on his part. I didn't even know him. He would soon be forced to resign for personal legal reasons that need not be dwelled on these years later.

Interim gubernatorial appointments were usually rubber-stamped when the General Assembly next convened. Governors need to keep the wheels of government going, and the need to make appointments continues while the part-time General Assembly is in recess. When lawmakers return to the capitol, interim picks are routinely approved in a block on the uncontested calendar. Wilder had given me an interim appointment to SCHEV. I had been warned about defying the powerful forces demanding that VMI be allowed to continue to violate the Constitution.

VMI had been ordered by the Fourth Circuit Court of Appeals to either admit women or develop a constitutionally acceptable compromise. VMI could, in theory, overcome the heavy constitutional presumption against the state spending all those millions on a public university reserved for males only. The good old boys came up with a plan to do just that. They rallied huge establishment and other political support for a program, hired the best lawyers in the country to plead their case in federal court and created a novel alliance with Mary Baldwin, a private liberal arts college for women located a short drive from VMI. VMI pitched a jointly run Virginia Women's Institute for Leadership: VMI alumni would fund the program, and it would be on par with VMI pedagogy and leadership training yet at a separate venue better suited for "the fairer sex." The Virginia Women's Institute for Leadership is still in existence at Mary Baldwin; I believe it is the only all-female cadet corps in the United States. I applaud them for doing it and for giving their students these opportunities. VMI rallied an impressive coalition of supporters—politicians and editorialists, women and men, new wave and old guard—with the legal talent to advocate for dualism in educational policy.

West Point had had female cadets since 1976, yet here we were, a generation later, refusing to face reality. Had Attorney General Terry simply enforced the Constitution, I believe she would have become not only governor but also a national figure. VMI folklore had loomed large when she was growing up. When it became a federal issue early in her term, she did not want to anger VMI's powerful political and fundraising apparatus.

As a lawyer, she had to know that separate but equal did not work in 1954, and it was not going to get different treatment from a Supreme Court featuring newly appointed Justice Ruth Bader Ginsburg. Whatever the Western District of Virginia might say, whatever the Fourth Circuit headquartered in Richmond might opine, Justice Ginsburg had to be convinced. No Supreme Court would buck on her equality of the sexes. Ginsburg had been right on equality for a long time; that is why she got appointed to the court.

I believe that I was the only lawyer on the council, but there may have been others. The members believed it was foolhardy for anyone on the council to defy the General Assembly, which at the time was supported by the broad coalition backing VMI. Nevertheless, the law was the law.

VMI's status as a public university meant SCHEV had to approve its proposal for the alliance with Mary Baldwin. Everyone understood the plan was an attempt to make a political end run around the Constitution.

I spoke at the final council discussion before voting. I can still see the room, hazy to be sure, but I can feel and hear my voice and see the reaction among the other members. I told them I understood why people felt they could not buck the powers that be. And yes, Governor Wilder supported the dual VMI and Mary Baldwin policy, as did the party's key players. But if I am afraid to speak out, then how could I criticize anyone else for not standing up?

VMI cadets. *Wikimedia Commons*.

"My views are known on these issues," I said. "They were known when I got appointed. I am quite certain the Supreme Court will rule that VMI must accept women or Virginia will do the right thing voluntarily."

I had studied the state's history. VMI had graduated one of history's greatest Americans, George Marshall, a five-star general during World War II and originator of the Marshall Plan. VMI had an illustrious history and many other distinguished graduates. Women had a constitutional right to attend VMI if the school remained a public university. End of story.

I was kicked off SCHEV. People like me, or women who wanted to attend VMI, did not know our place in the caste system. They never realized how Harry Byrd was getting the last laugh and how they all were being ruled from the grave.

10

RICHMOND'S ELECTED MAYOR LAW

C ities of Richmond's size invariably held direct mayoral elections, and Richmond's mayor had been elected citywide as recently as the late 1940s. But the growing civil rights movement made white powerbrokers realize that anti-Black voting laws were doomed. They changed to a council-elected mayor, which, by their theory, would at least prevent a "radical" from winning the office. Thus, never in Richmond's history had Black voters possessed the unfettered right to vote directly for their mayor.

Though the council post was ceremonial, Henry Marsh had become the first Black Richmonder to serve as mayor. He had been a longtime partner in a fabled civil rights law firm with Samuel Tucker and Oliver Hill.[16] After an extraordinary battle over land annexation and voting rights in which federal courts prevented new council elections for seven years, Marsh won the mayoralty in 1977 by a 5–4 vote split on racial lines.[17] Richmond's business and Republican establishment then used Marsh as a political punching bag. Marsh had many faults as mayor, but not the ones attributed to him by those antagonists. Racial politics had long been a way of life in Richmond. The white establishment, in true segregationist style, had used it to justify their superiority over all Black and white victims in the caste system.

Throughout the second half of the twentieth century, the mayor of Richmond had been appointed by city council from among its members, which by the 1990s numbered nine, each representing one council district.

In 1995, spurred by then-councilman Tim Kaine, council put on the ballot an advisory referendum asking voters whether they supported moving to a popularly elected mayor. Voters backed it by two to one. This change required amending the City Charter in the General Assembly.

No jurisdiction in Virginia was permitted home rule. The Byrd Machine had insisted on total control over localities on the chance a city like Richmond, Arlington or Norfolk might want to end segregation, fix its schools or reform any government aspect of local life. Charter changes required a two-thirds supermajority to pass. No proposed charter change opposed by a jurisdiction's state legislators had been approved, ever.

Wilder expressed reservations about Kaine's advisory referendum. He had a point: the referendum language did not include any details about the new office. The public had endorsed a concept. On the other hand, the job envisioned would be ceremonial, not powerful: a ribbon cutter, not an arm twister.

Opposition forces and unanswered questions did not make for the measure's smooth sailing in the General Assembly session of 1996. Now Senator Marsh and Delegate Dwight Jones ensured other members of the Richmond delegation did not go rogue on them. They got the political hot potato handed off to the House of Delegates' Committee on Cities, Counties and Towns, where Frank Hall, the senior legislator from Richmond, held sway as chair. He created a study committee led by Jones. Hall knew Jones intended to kill the measure, despite 2–1 public approval. Jones had been a longtime opponent of an elected mayor and found the current power structure to work fine for him and his cronies.

Richmond senator Joe Benedetti, a Republican, had a rivalry with Marsh. He managed to muscle his version of an elected mayor law onto the floor of the Senate for a vote. The Benedetti bill created a ceremonial mayor who had no vote on council or a veto. This mayor would preside over council meetings, put in legislation and be the face of the city. She or he could also vote to break council ties—rare in the nine-member body.[18]

The measure passed the Senate by a 21–19 vote. It was a toothless bill, but it kept an implicit promise to the voters. Every Democratic senator voted against it except one from Northern Virginia. When it got to the House, Chairman Hall gave it a polite burial by leading a 14–8 vote to continue it to the next year, whereupon he never called it up for another vote.[19]

In 1997, Hall's committee instead offered what was billed as a cleanup of the City Charter. This new and convoluted legislation was purportedly the first comprehensive review of the city's founding document in fifty years. It was a cleanup bill that did not include an elected mayor or, so far as I could tell, any useful reform to the corrupted half-century-old system of government. It was killed in a House Cities, Counties and Towns subcommittee by an unrecorded voice vote in 1997 and passed both houses nearly unanimously in 1998.[20] It may seem ironic that both white and Black elites favored this system. They had little in common but one overriding belief: they knew best, not the people.

Hall's legislative maneuverings seemingly put the issue to rest. I liked him and helped him win a tough primary during Wilder's governorship. There was no better Democrat than Frank Hall. He treated me with utmost kindness, as did his wife, Phoebe, a respected attorney. I respected him greatly, and he died too young. Hall was too savvy to buck Marsh, Jones and Wilder on the elected mayor law in the 1990s. The voters might have wanted to elect a mayor, but Hall and the Richmond Democratic establishment were not populists in that regard.

By the early 2000s, Wilder had become disgusted with the corruption and wastefulness of Richmond government. Kaine had been appointed mayor and then elected lieutenant governor. Lou Salomonsky, a local real estate developer, been charged with several felonies along with Councilmember Gwen Hedgepeth in a joint scandal that shocked city residents. Each would eventually serve prison time for engaging in criminal conduct.[21] I know Salomonsky and consider him my friend. He made a mistake. His wife is a wonderful person, and Salomonsky has rebuilt his life and business. I believe in redemption: America was founded and built by sinners in the eyes of the Europeans. Nevertheless, Salomonsky's conduct helped fuel the call to junk a corrupted form of government. The elected mayor concept again became viable.

Wilder told me Tom Bliley, a former Richmond mayor and congressman who was also a leader of the conservative business community, believed we could no longer afford the corrupt status quo. Wilder agreed, but for a different reason.

Some said Wilder's seemingly new position was hypocritical. But Wilder never had a problem with the concept of an elected mayor: his earlier critique was that the parameters of what that meant were not spelled out. Under the Kaine approach, the General Assembly got to define the job. Wilder thought it should be up to the people of Richmond. Richmond residents had not been offered this choice in the 1990s but felt the same.

A potential Wilder-Bliley Elected Mayor Commission still begged vital questions. How would the mayor be elected, and what would be his or her powers? Those were worthy of consideration once the threshold problem was solved; whatever reforms a commission might approve would go for naught unless the city council would recommend charter changes to the General Assembly. Wilder had no reason to assume the council would back any such proposal. Neither did I—quite the opposite.

Wilder and I discussed this practical problem. He had never partnered with Bliley in the past, so far as I could recall. Bliley represented the old guard, white establishment—Bliley would not disagree. He had been selected by the establishment to be mayor and eventually lost his position to Marsh. During Bliley's mayoral term, the white establishment had become increasingly nervous over the gains in Black voter registration. Back then, Richmond had a roughly 65 percent Black population; many were disenfranchised. New laws and activism meant the white caste system would soon no longer dominate Richmond elections. There was more than racism; businessmen gained financially from sweetheart city contracts.

Bliley was the leader in using annexation to play the ultimate political hardball. They cut a deal to annex vast tracts of rural land south of the James River that was then part of Chesterfield County. This was a racially motivated land grab, unique even to a city so long defined by black-and-white politics. A majority Black city would suddenly have a white majority voter registration base. As noted, this unprecedented racial annexation caused political havoc, causing the courts to block elections for years, an amazing story masterfully recounted in another book.[22] Bliley became despised as the white man who had for years blocked Black voters from regaining their rightful place in city politics through a procedure straight from the nineteenth century. Ray Boone, famed editor of the Black-owned *Richmond Free Press*, held Bliley in maximum low regard, as the saying goes.

It thus seemed inconceivable that Wilder and Bliley would ally. When Wilder first mentioned the possibility, I only knew the retired congressman as a Republican opponent: a conservative, not a reactionary, though I did not know the history from thirty-five years ago. True, cutting a deal across the political aisle might be rare, but it fell within the normative spectrum of politics. Joining with former Mayor Bliley did not seem a bridge too far; it seemed a bold political stroke.

I remember Wilder asking me to meet him and Bliley for lunch at the Country Club of Virginia. I did not fully appreciate the scene until later. "The Club" accepted its first Black member in 1992, years into Wilder's gubernatorial term.[23] As for Bliley: he did not prove the stereotype I expected. If he had blinked—and he had his arm twisted by key elements of the old guard—the elected mayor push would have failed. His support would ultimately prove indispensable. Neither Wilder nor Bliley had a magic wand for how to pass it through council. We calculated that all the political roads led to a dead end.

———◆———

SHORTLY THEREAFTER I ENCOUNTERED Rita Henderson outside the entrance to Capitol Square. I met Rita and her brother, Arnold, an attorney, during the Wilder campaigns. She knew more than I had forgotten about Richmond politics. I asked whether she remembered Hall putting a referendum provision in his City Charter bill in 1998. I had a vague recollection of such a provision. Henderson suggested I go online and check it out. Internet research had not yet become second nature to me or many of my contemporaries. I still did research in the library, as I had since grade school.

I picked up Thomas after school at Mary Munford Elementary, and he and I did our homework together. Buried in twenty-two pages of Hall's bill language stood a new charter provision, Section 3.06.1.[24] This clause created a right for any citizen to lead a petition drive for the purpose of changing the City Charter. There were technical requirements, and some matters were off limits, but bypassing city council to change the mayor from appointed to elected could be achieved by a citizen referendum.

If the legal language could be worked out, it would take a petition signed by Richmond voters numbering "ten percent or more of the largest number of votes cast in any general or primary election held in the city during the five years immediately preceding" the petition. The required number seemed impossible: it would be the most voter signatures ever gathered in any jurisdiction in the state. To get on the ballot for president or governor, a candidate needs to collect ten thousand verified voter signatures statewide. We would need more than that just from Richmond. The law said 10 percent, but given the Richmond Registrar's record of being the biggest signature disqualifier in the state, that likely meant 15 percent or more of the residents would need to sign. On a per capita basis, we would need to collect the equivalent of 300,000 signatures statewide to put a referendum on the ballot in November 2003. Unprecedented to my knowledge.

The path had a unique twist. Any charter change approved by voters was sent to the General Assembly as if sent by council. Hall had given Richmonders an end run around an ossified council.

The provision had one other bombshell. The advisory referendum in 1995 had posed a broad question, but now, the citizen petition had to show, word for word, the precise language to be added to the charter. Any referendum sent to the General Assembly would face an up or down vote on a concrete proposal. There would be no carte blanche given the General Assembly to change things. They could kill it legally. But no member of the Richmond delegation would so brazenly risk the voters' wrath.

How, then, to draft the referendum to include every detail of the mayor's office, powers and duties?

Wilder and Bliley formed their commission. There would be nine other voting members, each representing one of Richmond's council districts. Bliley realized Wilder would take the lead, and Wilder picked all the members. They were citizens, not the usual politicos. The co-executive directors were Boyd Marcus, the former congressman's trusted political consultant, and me. Once the members agreed on the specifics of the mayor's office, McGuireWoods, the mega law firm, would draft the raw product into legislative form.

We held meetings across the city that fall. Marcus had to back out when Congressman Eric Cantor, who had worked for Bliley and won his Seventh District seat after Bliley retired, ran into staffing problems and needed a new chief of staff. There were many ideas worth debating. The members had nine different opinions on the scope of the mayor's powers, but consensus was gradually beginning to form.

The make-or-break issue involved the process for electing the mayor. If the commission got it wrong, the referendum would be unviable. There were two plans put forward at the commission's initial meeting. Plan A straightforwardly defined the winning candidate as the one who received the most votes. A runoff requirement between the top two candidates if no one secured a majority had merit and guaranteed a new mayor would enter office with majority support. The citizen commission members said a plurality should suffice, as did Wilder and Bliley.

My job as executive director did not end at the research or policy side. McGuireWoods was not pro bono counsel; its lawyers charged hundreds of dollars an hour and had been promised $20,000 to write the final charter change proposal. This was at a reduced rate but still not cheap. Fortunately, I knew Voting Rights Act jurisprudence. Some states at the time used a 40 percent threshold for purposes of requiring a runoff. If no candidate got a 40 percent plurality, then a runoff was held between the two candidates receiving the most votes. The 40 percent triggers predated the Voting Rights Act and had been folded into the proposal as part of the political compromise needed to pass it. Richmond's history of racial bloc voting made the runoff provision illegal under the Voting Rights Act. The registration rolls might be majority Black, but the turnout in council elections amounted to a 60 percent white majority. The Voting Rights Act thus presumed a white candidate would win any runoff 60–40.

Richmond's Black leadership opposed any straight popular vote or runoff procedure, which they suspected the city's white leadership wanted to guarantee a white mayor. A loose group of individuals developed a unique proposal: the victor should be the candidate carrying the majority of the city's nine council districts, a mini electoral college. Then, as now, five districts were majority Black, three were majority white, and one, the Fifth, was plurality Black.[25] This idea gained traction among the city's Black leaders.

The white business community and politicians were equally adamant in the other direction. They believed the five-of-nine equation guaranteed the election of a Black mayor. The white leadership laid down their marker: the mayor must be the person winning the popular vote. There would be no mini electoral college. One person, one vote, no compromise.

I must confess that despite my—at that time nearly thirty years— involvement in Virginia politics, the level of racial distrust between the leaders of the white and Black communities continually astounded me. Segregation's legacy lingers in a way that I do not think I can ever understand.

Wilder asked the members to indicate their preference between the mini electoral college and popular vote systems. The commission split 6–5 in favor of the popular vote, which Wilder and Bliley both favored. They had spent their lives in politics winning and helping win elections based on the popular vote. I favored the popular vote as well. I knew a Black candidate could win the popular vote in Richmond and that anyone who said differently did not know the voting statistics. We all knew the history of the electoral college, which was devised to get states like Virginia to support the Constitution. We were all comfortable with the one person, one vote principle. As the commission's work continued, I remained confident those wedded to the electoral college system would eventually agree to go with the popular vote. But the divisions hardened.

I have a vague recollection of Marty Jewell first bringing the following idea to me. He would be elected to council in 2004 and prove to be someone who had an open mind on policy and always wanted to have a factual debate. I respect Marty. But, back then, I did not know him and did not pay enough attention when he initially brought the idea to me.

A member of the commission asked me to meet with two professors, John Moeser from Virginia Commonwealth University and Tom Shields from the University of Richmond. We met at Ellwood Thompson's, the town's best health food restaurant. Dr. Shields was to my right, and Dr. Moeser was taking the lead across from me. To me, he was just some professor and his sidekick with an idea, two academics with no political experience. I did not know Moeser had earned a reputation for being a leading expert on urban policy and was well respected around the country, not merely in Richmond. The professors said they had been meeting with people on all sides of the election argument. They said they gamed out a solution.

To win the mayoral election, a candidate would need to win both the popular vote and a majority of the nine council districts. This seemed to cut the Gordian knot. On its face, who could object? In discussing the matter with them, I realized why my view of the voting statistics differed from others. Everyone else was basing their analysis on past city council elections, which the white establishment had always held in the spring. They were tantamount to off-year elections. This explained why projections showed the typical council turnout was 60 percent white.

Wilder and Bliley wanted to hold the mayor's election on the same ballot as the presidential race. The professors were armed with an equally compelling truth: they felt a straight popular vote would never be acceptable to the city's Black leadership, ever. All I could offer were projections, analysis, computer printouts. People had made up their minds, and the statistics would not matter. They were going to stick to the history they knew. Why not just do what the professors and Marty Jewell wanted?

The white establishment knew their own history and insisted that a white candidate could never win five of nine council districts. The 1970s annexation of the white exurban-rural citizens in Chesterfield had been a plan hatched by "a small, but powerful group of white 'Virginia gentlemen' who met secretly for several years, plotting how to maintain white control of Virginia's capital as it was becoming increasingly black," as Moeser summarized the powerbrokers' motivation in the *Richmond Times-Dispatch* nearly fifty years later.[26] The Supreme Court would later condemn this annexation as unconstitutional in *Richmond v. United States* (1975), but the justices also found the racial toothpaste of annexation already out of the tube, so to speak. They needed a practical remedy to the wrong and ordered that the existing method of at-large election to city council, which advantaged the white majority, be changed to the current nine district system. The court divided the city into four districts where a white candidate figured to win, four districts where a black candidate figured to win and one swing district. The next council elected chose Marsh as mayor. White leaders felt the five of nine system amounted to guaranteeing a Black mayor.

Neither side would budge. You would need to give both what they wanted. But if racial block existed, then a fight between a Black candidate and a white candidate would always end in a stalemate, the former winning the majority of districts and the latter winning the popular vote. In theory, there could be many candidates, but political logic suggested each side would realize a multicandidate field would split their own voters and, at the least, might lead to unpredictable results. Political pressure would therefore lead to a two-person race in the end, with each racial bloc backing its favored candidate. This is precisely what we needed to avoid. Their proposal, if you accepted their logic, guaranteed no clear winner no matter how or if you had runoff. I thanked them. Like Bobby Fischer, I had to go home, take out the political chess board and study where I had gone wrong.

WHATEVER PLAN THE COMMISSION might recommend, it would need to be put to a referendum. We were pitching the elected mayor law as a way to bring people together. If the white and Black communities were clearly split on the plan, it would lack legitimacy even if it received a majority vote.

We needed a show of unity. I delved further into the Voting Rights Act. The law was clear: changing from an appointed mayor to an elected mayor would be evaluated in comparison with the 62 percent white vote in previous elections. That struck me as wrong, but it did seem to be the law.

I saw that the popular vote option was an illusion. President Bush would be seeking reelection in 2004. If everything went smoothly, a new elected mayor law would be enacted in that spring. Bush would not want to get into a controversy between white and Black Richmonders that close to the election in a state he needed to win. His Justice Department appointees would therefore reject any straight-up popular vote law. It would be declared illegal any way you sliced it.

The mini electoral college system harbored a hidden benefit. The "one person one vote" mandate enshrined by *Baker v. Carr* (1962) required all nine districts to contain roughly the same population. The white areas of the city were more affluent, and their citizens registered and voted more regularly than citizens in the less affluent districts. The voting differences were dramatic. The city's wealthiest district, the First in the West End, was more than 90 percent white and had the same rough population as the poorest district, the 85 percent Black and Latino Ninth in Southside.[27] In the 2000 presidential election, First District voters cast roughly 11,500 votes, and those from the

Ninth cast roughly 6,000.[28] The district with the third-highest percentage of white voters, the Fourth, which had been annexed from Chesterfield in the 1970s, cast around 10,750 votes; the second-poorest district, the Sixth in the Central Business District and nearby low-rent housing, cast around 3,800. (The Second had the second-highest percentage of white residents, but its location around VCU made it unique in Richmond as a majority-white progressive district with low turnout and unpredictable results.)

The combined popular vote and five-of-nine system had a practical problem: who makes the runoff if no candidate wins both the popular vote and five council districts outright? Assume there are three candidates each winning three districts: logic would say the top two vote-getters would go to the runoff. But what if two candidates lead the others in the number of districts won and two other candidates have a greater popular vote?

Hanging over this practical problem loomed the Voting Rights Act. The law did not guarantee a particular outcome: if the candidate favored by the Black community finished last, so be it, provided the election system was fair. However, the runoff provision would need to satisfy the act standing alone. As I read the law, it protected the freedom of choice long denied the Black majority in Richmond, indeed, across the South. At all times, the Black community has the option, as the Voting Rights Act views it, of pooling resources to back a single candidate that they feel best advocates for their interests. Federal law requires that this candidate have a fair chance and that any change in the election process does not dilute the Black communities' power to elect their single candidate. No candidate has a right to win: they might be a lousy campaigner, wrong on the issues, face secular political headwinds and so on.

Moreover, important in Richmond is that the white community would believe its candidate, if campaigns indeed divided on racial lines, also had a fair shot. The Voting Rights Act did not require this, but we needed a big, politically unified vote in support of the proposed change.

Wilder and Bliley had the respect of the body. When they both explained their support for the five-of-nine system, any opposition faded away. The use of the popular vote to determine the runoff candidates further cemented support. We had a deal.

———————

WITH THE ELECTION IMBROGLIO settled, the commission moved quickly to resolve the powers and duties of the mayor. They were sharp disagreements at first, but accommodation to reach a consensus proved doable. We all agreed to keep further details on the vote private, and I am bound to respect that today. The commission voted 10–1 for the final proposal. The *Richmond Times-Dispatch* announced in bold headlines that the commission had recommended an elected mayor.

A summons came for me to meet Gordon Rainey, the chairman at Hunton and Williams (now Hunton Andrews Kurth), the city's other premier law firm. I do not recall previously meeting him. He greeted me like a conquering hero. I had done the city a great service, he said. We needed an elected mayor. Everyone in the law firm sends their regards, Paul. In the days of King Arthur, I veritably would have been offered his daughter's hand in marriage.

I received a phone call from him a few days later. I went from the Round Table to having my head on a spike. He had apparently not read the news article or the details of the plan. Upon discovering the five-of-nine system lurking in the news stories, Gordon and his colleagues were now unhappy. He thought the elected mayor proposal was a bad idea for Richmond.

I started to get calls from business and other leaders of the white establishment expressing similar disappointment. They vowed to make certain it never became law.

Now Senator Marsh and the white establishment invariably took opposing sides. But here they were proof of the oldest political adage: the enemy of my enemy is my friend. The old guard from both races started working to kill the Wilder-Bliley Commission plan.

About a month later, the phone rang again, this time from McGuireWoods, the law firm hired to put the charter changes proposed into proper form. Truth be told, it is possible that it was Richard Cullen, McGuireWoods chairman, on the line, but I am more confident in saying it was Frank Atkinson. We knew each other from politics over the years. He had been a top campaign aide to Marshall Coleman and a major player in Governor George Allen's administration. His books on Virginia politics are considered required reading by those interested in knowing the history of the state's politics from the perspective of one of top GOP consultants in Virginia history.[29] Atkinson is also a competent attorney, a major reason the consulting arm of McGuireWoods has achieved great success over the years. He had been initially eager to help both Wilder and Bliley.

Atkinson (or Cullen) said the firm could no longer participate. The law firm had determined drafting such a measure would be impossible, he said, given all the local, state and federal legal hurdles to clear.

The job was tricky. It might be a political bridge too far and take Houdini to get the measure ultimately enacted into law given all the opposition and trapdoors lurking in the future. But legally impossible to draft? No way. This was an excuse developed to cover a withdrawal under pressure from the establishment.

I informed Wilder. No problem, Paul. Just add it to your list of responsibilities as executive director.

⸺ ✦ ⸺

As I BEGAN THE process of drafting the charter change, there was waning support for the measure. It did not take a Geiger counter to sense less enthusiasm in more and more quarters. In terms of chronology, I cannot with absolute certainty recall nearly twenty years later which of the following events took place first. But the timing is less important than the gauntlets thrown at the charter change.

Bliley brought the business community on board, and its leaders and corporations had put up the initial money to fund the commission. But after the proposal was announced, the funders soured on the elected mayor plan.

At some point, there was a meeting in the boardroom of Virginia Union, now Virginia Union University. I can still see us sitting around the room in comfortable chairs. VU had long been a pillar in the community and a close ally of Wilder, its most famous alumnus. His papers are there, though his gubernatorial records are with the other governors' at the Library of Virginia.[30]

During the meeting, I realized several people on the commission wanted to postpone the referendum until next year. I took some criticism from the speakers; my recollection is that James Sheffield, a retired Richmond Circuit Court judge, was most strongly in favor of waiting until next year. He was a close friend of Wilder who had earned an extraordinary level of respect within the community. He was a great lawyer who in 1974 became Virginia's first Black judge since Reconstruction.[31] Knowing Judge Sheffield, I am certain his views were sincerely held. At the same time, he could scarcely be considered a babe in the political woods. He would not have spoken out without the blessing of key players in the Black establishment.

I disagreed. It was true that we faced increasing opposition from establishment detractors, but we had momentum. The best way to kill a referendum is to delay it.

I do not recall Bliley being at the meeting, but Wilder played his cards close to the vest. He thanked everyone and said he would take everything under advisement. We talked after the meeting, and he seemed surprised by Sheffield's effort to delay the referendum. He intended to move forward, but the daunting signature requirements were a concern. We had no immediate solution.

Bliley asked Wilder to meet. I remember driving there; Wilder told me to wait outside, and he recounted to me later what happened. I believe he said Boyd Marcus was there, though it could have been GOP strategist Ray Allen, or perhaps even both of them. Bliley had apparently gotten word that John Stewart Bryan III, patriarch of the family that had owned the *Richmond Times-Dispatch* for three generations and its then-chairman, had decided to position the paper against the proposal.[32] The publisher, like other prominent members of the white business establishment, felt the plan guaranteed a Black mayor. This, apparently, they could not abide. This would have been a body blow to our hopes in the white community. We already faced opposition from Ray Boone in his *Free Press*. The political walls were beginning to close in.

Wilder had been growing frustrated with the temerity displayed by leaders on both sides of the opposition. Bliley was the connection to the white establishment, which was clearly pressuring him to break with Wilder. In that regard, Bliley owed Wilder nothing; they had not been aligned in politics over the years. Bliley understood the realities of the newspaper's position, but he felt the commission had done good work. Bliley still felt the elected mayor law would benefit Richmond. He had no intention of deserting Wilder—quite the opposite. They would go have a showdown with Bryan.

The leaders had their sit-down not long thereafter. It is possible others were at the meeting, but if there were, I do not know. Bryan said that he intended to have the editorial board publicly oppose the measure. Wilder said Bliley kept his word and strongly backed the referendum plan. The former governor said the plan helped the city. It was needed sooner or later. If Bryan went public in this way, it would likely kill the effort. Wilder and Bliley called Bryan's bluff. Wilder said he would hold a press conference if Bryan moved forward discussing the meeting and say he had tried to help but could not do any more, the citizens were now on their own.

I asked Wilder whether he thought Bryan had the guts to do it. He said no. "This was 2003," Wilder said. "He cannot get into that kind of public fight with me, not over this." No one would be fooled as to the true reason for his opposition. The *Times-Dispatch* could not recover from such a stance, nor could Bryan. Thus Wilder did not consider Bryan a threat. Bryan blinked.

THE DAUNTING TASK OF collecting signatures loomed larger. Wilder said the business community would not front the money for signature gathering. Bliley still believed he could raise money through calls and direct mail appeals, but that was not likely to generate enough to fund the signature collecting we believed was needed. Wilder asked me what I wanted to do.

"I'll put up the money," I said. Then I shot my mouth off to the press, gloating about how easy it would be to get the signatures. I became campaign manager in 1985 by talking over my skis. Now eighteen years later, it was déjà vu all over again.

Getting the signatures would be arduous given the dearth of available help for the project. I had never run a charter referendum petition drive, nor had anyone else in Richmond.

My new role as signature collector-in-chief started in mid-June. We had to move fast and would need to pay circulators. Some would accept a check; others wanted cash and carry and would only give me their petition sheets when I forked over cash. I paid $1.00 to $2.50 per signature depending on the circulator's negotiating skills. I paid more to my best people. We did some advertising, made signs, printed thousands of petition sheets, sent out mailings—the usual campaign fundamentals.

A pressing reality quickly dawned on me. Richmond Circuit Court controlled the citizen-initiative referendum process, and the petition sheets with the required petitions were given to Richmond Circuit Court Clerk Bevill Dean.[33] I have tremendous respect for him and his successor and protégé, Ed Jewett. The Clerk's Office had to verify the signatures, but only the Richmond Registrar had the apparatus to do so.

Richmond Registrar Kirk Showalter had a well-earned reputation for disqualifying signatures most other registrars would have accepted. While she did not resist the referendum, she did not volunteer to be helpful, either. The registrar refused to review any signatures without a court order.

We would need to have all our signatures to the clerk by early August to guarantee the registrar would have time to review them and then the court enough time to order the referendum be held and the language printed on the November ballots.

Dean made a good suggestion to run the process efficiently. When filing the order to compel Showalter to count the signatures on an expedited basis, I should likewise ask the court to further order her to provide a running count. Chief Judge Melvin Hughes agreed, and he set up a useful counting process. By noon every Friday, I would submit to the court, through the clerk, all the petitions containing signatures ready to be counted. Cecelia Hargrove, then a deputy clerk, was assigned by Dean to be the go-to person for the petition handoffs. She could not have been nicer. She is now the chief deputy, in line to run for the clerk's spot when Jewett retires. We had roughly seven weeks to get twelve thousand signatures.

Opponents, led by Senator Marsh, mocked our chances of getting them by the cutoff date. They told people not to waste their time helping us. Sowing doubt was smart politics on his part. He and his allies held sway with key councilmembers.

I talked to Jim Ukrop, whose family ran the renowned Ukrop's Super Markets. Many business owners were leery of getting their businesses involved in political issues. Unlike most of them, he backed the commission plan. He had promised when the commission was formed to let petitioners stand outside his stores. I reminded him of his promise.

During this period, the business community had been twisting arms on city council to get a meals tax increase to pay for what would become the Dominion Energy Center for the Performing Arts. Ukrop was the biggest advocate for the proposed Arts Center outside of the arts community itself. He said he could not risk letting people petition at Ukrop's while the antireferendum council had a life-or-death hold on the Arts Center. But he said that after council voted in July, the stores were all mine, the managers would do anything I wanted except give me free food. Had he reneged on the promise, I doubt we could have gotten the signatures in time. It was a gutsy, classy move. The city is in his debt.

At the time, Ukrop's stores were all closed on Sundays, unlike their rivals. This allowed the Kroger across the street from the Carytown Ukrop's to do a colossal Sunday business—the best location in Richmond to get good signatures on Sunday. Unlike Jim Ukrop, I could not afford to take a Sunday off from petitioning. But Kroger's national policy banned petitioning on store property. My needs in that regard were rather small: I would stand to the side of the main entrance doors and then politely ask for signatures, only on Sundays. I called the CEO of Kroger every day for weeks.

There came a time when the Kroger CEO decided to take my call. I guess he wanted to find out who the heck refused to take no for an answer. He agreed to let me petition at the Carytown store on Sundays only. "Does that mean you will stop calling now?" he joked. "No promises," I answered. He laughed.

Several young operatives needed summer employment, and a good petition circulator can make $800 a week. Unfortunately, they all lived in Henrico or Chesterfield, not Richmond. I knew Registrar Showalter would check their residence status: a circulator must swear before a notary that he or she is a resident of that locality and Virginia law required all circulators of local referendums to be registered voters in that jurisdiction. That is actually unconstitutional, and had there been more time, I might have gone to federal court. However, there was nothing in the law prohibiting them from switching their registrations to Richmond even if the primary motive rested on circulating petitions. I told them the law and their options. Soon they were picking up petitions to circulate as the newest registered voters in the city.

They were all Republican or GOP-leaning, except for my top paid petitioner, libertarian Bob Lynch. He is a long-time city resident who travels the country as a professional petitioner. Sloppy petitioners would cost more money in the long run through signatures being invalidated. Lynch charged more, but he earned every penny with a tremendous work ethic. He had a white beard and the friendliest eyes and smile that he could utilize to coax almost anyone into signing a petition. He also insisted on reading the charter change and peppered me with questions before agreeing to be a circulator. He had to support a petition before becoming a circulator.

As a technical matter, state law only required a Richmond voter to sign her or his name on the petition. But the Richmond registrar would not count a lone signature as a qualified voter signature. Her reasoning was that it would be impossible to tell whether the person was on the books as a Richmond voter. It could be anyone from any state with the same name as someone registered in Richmond, or there might be more than one individual registered in Richmond under the same name. How could her office know which John Smith had signed? At least, that was her position. She could have asked her employees to check the signature on the petition against the voter signature cards. Richmond is not New York City. How long would it take to go to the alphabetically filed petition cards and find the matching John Smith?

I do not believe the registrar appreciated the importance of the rights she was being paid to protect. She seemed to believe the right to sign a petition, or the right to get on the ballot, rested with her, not the Constitution, nor common sense. To me, the political rights guaranteed by the laws of the state are sacred. Yet Showalter's rules ruled. This underscored the importance of the circulator ensuring a voter clearly signed his or her name and full address.

Bob Lynch understood this. He also had a great sense of where to collect signatures. I remember the first time I collected signatures at a summer shindig on Brown's Island among swarms of people on a gorgeous weekend afternoon. I circulated in the crowd for hours. Another day I stood outside the bridge to the island as those going to a concert strolled by. I collected hundreds more signatures. But, as Bob predicted, a big percentage would prove to be disqualified. When we asked someone if they were a Richmond voter and wanted to sign a petition, many citizens living in the surrounding counties would say yes. Their addresses were indeed Richmond, Virginia, but they were thinking of Greater Richmond rather than municipal lines. Despite best intentions, only those who lived within city limits were qualified signatories.

Lynch played an indispensable role in the elected mayor project. He is a fine individual who worked hard and helped his city. We likely would not have collected enough signatures without him.

———————

Marsh and the city's white and Black establishments were growing more vehemently against the referendum proposal. Wilder stayed in the background and let me be the public face of the petition drive.

I was always fond of playing political chess. I decided a good move would be to toss a little misdirection at our opponents. When we filed our first week's petitions with the registrar, I held back a chunk of the petitions and intentionally understated our progress. We did the same the next Friday. Our lagging numbers also allowed supporters to sound the proverbial alarm, which got us more workers. Soon the grapevine had Marsh and business leaders chuckling about how we were too disorganized to get the job done. Even Wilder heard the news.

I told Wilder about the game we were playing. "Henry is lucky we gave him that seat," I said, knowing Doug would laugh. Ten years earlier, he and I had fought hard to create the majority-Black district that Marsh now represented.

It was hard work, and the paid guys were tired from pounding the summer pavement day after day, but we were cooking with gas, as my mom liked to say. I enjoyed getting the signatures, talking to people, learning what they were thinking. Marty Jewell still had his reservations about the plan and took heat from other activists, but he helped enormously.

The opposition had a press conference during the summer, with several speakers making ridiculous, race-baiting claims that I will not repeat. Having worked for Howell, then Wilder, then Mark Warner, I had yet to see this side of politics aimed at me personally. It disgusted me. We got the signatures.

The Black establishment had uniformly come out against the referendum by the fall. They likely spent more money in direct mail and radio advertisements urging people to Vote No than our Vote Yes campaign. Think of it: all the commission wanted to do was give Black Richmonders their first-ever right to directly vote for mayor, the same right enjoyed by citizens in almost every city of our size in the United States. Furthermore, the five-of-nine system had been created to ensure that working-class Black citizens had the full power of their vote.

They said our proposal was anti-Black. Wilder told me not to worry. I knew they were selling wolf tickets, as we used to say in my VISTA days, but still, they should have been ashamed of themselves. They were attacking me because I was white and Jewish.

When the *Times-Dispatch* asked me to write a column explaining the proposal, it practically wrote itself. Richmond had been two cities for too long. We needed to finally have a system where all voters, of all identities, would vote in an election where one leader would emerge chosen by all.

The people agreed on Election Day.

The final tally showed the referendum getting over 80 percent, as close to unanimous as one can get in a heated political contest. We carried 90 percent of the city's precincts, and the few we lost were by narrow margins.

Those seeing the results may figure we had a cakewalk. But without Wilder's credibility, the false attacks rooted in racial politics would have created a split in which the white community largely supported the measure while the Black community largely rejected it. The referendum still would have passed, given Richmond's turnout in an off-year election, but Marsh and Jones knew they could kill the measure in the General Assembly with that split in the popular vote.

The huge margin of victory ensured General Assembly passage the next year. The General Assembly had never backed a charter change when the elected lawmakers from that jurisdiction opposed the proposal. Jones became a sponsor of the final legislation, a smart move on his part.

In the 2004 General Assembly that spring, only five lawmakers, all Republicans, voted against the measure in the final vote. Lieutenant Governor Tim Kaine and his staff deserve a lot of credit for that vote. Delegate Viola Baskerville, a former Richmond City councilperson, was the lead sponsor of the bill. She has done a lot for Richmond over the years. I voted for her when she ran in the Democratic lieutenant governor primary the following year, when she placed second out of four candidates.

The lopsided endorsement, with all the state's Black legislators now on board, ensured approval from the Department of Justice. Its lawyers had been initially skeptical the change satisfied the Voting Rights Act. Wilder and I traveled to Washington by train to meet with them. I recall presenting our opening legal analysis and answering some of their questions. This was only par for the course; regardless, the VRA required the Justice Department to review any change, whether challenged or not. I had written a legal memo to counter a civil right challenge filed by a citizen or group whose name escapes me. This was a high-profile matter, and DOJ needed to show a thorough analysis. But President Bush wanted smooth sailing this election year.

Wilder's reputation preceded him. They knew he was not pulling some sleight of hand on the voters in his native city.

We returned from Washington to face TV cameras at the train station. There were smiles of confidence all around. Making history is fun, even if it was way harder than it should have been.

THERE HAVE NOW BEEN five elections under the elected mayor law, and all the winners were Black. In the 2020 election, the three top candidates were Black and the only white candidate got 7 percent.

In the history of Richmond's elected mayor, only one white candidate ever had a chance. City council president Bill Pantele had terrific credentials. He had a good record, money and campaign experience and is a very likeable guy. He got 32 percent of the vote and carried three of the city's nine council districts. The winner of that race was none other than Delegate Dwight Jones.

Marsh, Jones and others condemning in racial terms the electoral reform the whole city wanted is all that is wrong with identity politics. If the white guy who helped Wilder win can be so falsely attacked, then no white person is free from that stuff.

I refuse to buy into the segregationist mindset that made everyone either white or Black. I don't see politics that way. Wilder is Wilder, Kaine is Kaine, Warner is Warner; we agree on some things, we don't agree on others. You do not have to love everybody, but I remember Reverend Jackson's mantra, "I am somebody." Jackson and I were not political allies, but he was right on that point. We are all somebody, and you need to demand respect on that basis. If you will not demand it, do not count on anyone giving it to you.

The racial lie would have won if Wilder had not been there backstopping the Vote YES on the elected mayor referendum election. Wilder's leadership made the whole long battle from start to finish possible. Wilder was the leader, which is not to take away the great contributions of everyone else. Wilder, Kaine, former congressman Bliley, the Wilder-Bliley Commission and, ultimately, the people of Richmond, called the establishment's bluff and won.

11

YOUNGKIN'S CLOSE WIN

White Backlash and Black Paternalism

National Democratic leaders are playing a phony race card by claiming a white backlash powered Republican Glen Youngkin's upset win in Virginia's 2021 gubernatorial election. Doug Wilder knows better. He has increasingly believed Democratic leaders, in Virginia and nationally, have been insultingly taking Black voters for granted. Barack Obama and Joe Biden shrugged him off, as did the Democratic National Committee, Terry McAuliffe and the Virginia Democratic Party establishment. They therefore missed Wilder's important insight.

From 1970 through 1976, the two major parties in Virginia struggled to redefine themselves as the conservative Byrd Machine faded into oblivion. Independent candidates won three-way statewide contests in 1970, 1971 and 1976. Howell's racially diverse progressive coalition pushed the Democratic Party to the left. In turn, rural Byrd Democrats joined conservative suburbanites to move the Virginia GOP further right. The crosswise migration had been completed by the 1977 gubernatorial general election. Since then, the major parties have won every statewide office. No independent has even mounted a serious challenge.

Viewed through this new prism, Youngkin's victory fits neatly into this forty-four-year-old pattern. No gubernatorial candidate of the sitting president's party has garnered 50 percent of the vote. All have lost except Democrat Terry McAuliffe in 2013. He won the closest gubernatorial contest in a generation with 47.7 percent of the total vote.

In 2013, McAuliffe ran as a "Virginia Democrat," a strategy honed by Wilder, Warner, Robb and others. But McAuliffe wanted a "national Democrat" narrative in 2021, seeing the bogeyman of Donald Trump as his ticket back to the Governor's Mansion. A respected Watson Center Poll, published less than four months before the primary, showed him garnering only 26 percent, with fully 49 percent of Democratic voters undecided. For McAuliffe, essentially the incumbent in the race with broad name recognition, this showed no enthusiasm for another McAuliffe term even among Democrats. Three Black opponents, including two female legislators barely known statewide, collectively amassed nearly the same vote.

McAuliffe desperately needed a powerful issue. At the time, President Biden maintained an impressive approval rating. He had carried Virginia with 54.1 percent, the biggest Democratic presidential margin since 1944. Incumbent governor Ralph Northam in 2017, Senator Tim Kaine in 2018 and Senator Warner in 2020 all had cruised to victory. Trump got only 44 percent both in 2016 and 2020. The Virginia Democratic Party establishment wanted McAuliffe to win the primary.

Party strategists believed State Senator Amanda Chase had a lock on the GOP gubernatorial nomination. The self-described "Trump in Heels" played maskless to boisterous crowds on the campaign trial. Chase led the early GOP polls. Republican Party infighting over the choice of nomination process seemed likely to benefit her prospects.

McAuliffe knew Democratic voters' fear of Trump could be redirected to Chase. Using her as the face of the Trump bogeyman had strategic advantages. The more McAuliffe could make the election about who could be best trusted to stop a gun-toting Trump worshipper from becoming governor, the less primary voters would focus on his inability to articulate a compelling narrative for his return to the Governor's Mansion.

The 2020 social justice protests made white Democrats, especially the growing number of millennial and youth voters, increasingly attuned to racial issues. The party longed to make racial history in 2021. By focusing on Trump, the McAuliffe campaign blunted this strong impulse.

Democratic leaders dismissed Youngkin as a possible GOP nominee despite his estimated $400 million net worth. They had forgotten history. In 1978, John Warner, married to a similarly well-off Elizabeth Taylor, won a U.S. Senate seat in his first campaign. Wealthy car dealer Don Beyer likewise triumphed in his first political foray, capturing the lieutenant governorship in 1989. Mark Warner used his estimated $200 million telecom fortune to secure the Democratic gubernatorial nomination and defeat the Republican nominee in 2001. McAuliffe likewise used his tens of millions to dominate the bankrupt Democrats after their state ticket got crushed in the 2009 landslide loss. This investment earned him an uncontested gubernatorial nomination four years later.

The GOP had not won a statewide race for twelve years. They were a party with little money and less credibility statewide. Youngkin, like Warner and McAuliffe, had the resources to buy the nomination. Virginia history said he should not be underestimated.

Even more importantly, Virginia politics had become increasingly partisan on Election Day. The Youngkin ticket's sweep of all three statewide office marked the fourth straight election where one party ran the table. The unofficial vote count showed Youngkin winning with 1,663,596 votes (50.6 percent), running mate Winsome Sears garnering 1,658,767 (50.7 percent) and GOP attorney general nominee Jason Miyares amassing 1,647,534 votes (50.4 percent). There was barely 0.3 percent of the vote separating the three. (Youngkin receiving more votes but a lower percentage of the vote than Sears is due to the fact that 18,164 people voted for governor while leaving the lieutenant governor line blank.)

Prior to Youngkin, every winning Republican gubernatorial nominee in the two-party era won in a landslide: John Dalton in 1977 (55.9 percent), George Allen in 1993 (58.3 percent), Jim Gilmore in 1997 (55.8 percent) and Bob McDonnell in 2009 (58.6 percent).

Virginia has become a much more Democratic state since 2009. Youngkin had no chance to win in such a landslide. But if Youngkin's wealth could help unite his party, a strong straight ticket vector might create reverse coattails. In that regard, Youngkin's team ran a brilliant campaign. They were newcomers to Virginia gubernatorial politics. Historically, outsiders have gravitated to losing national themes. Youngkin's team avoided this newcomer mistake. In business terms, they urged people to "buy locally."

McAuliffe's willingness to be depicted as a "national Democrat" is therefore baffling. His team knew Virginia political history. The different campaign mindsets are encapsulated by the education issue. McAuliffe allowed his education policy to be depicted as driven by elected and appointed government officials. He became the candidate of the government, historically fatal in Virginia. In contrast, Youngkin positioned himself as the candidate whose education policy valued parents, not politicians or bureaucrats.

It is important to see through the media mania over Youngkin's upset victory: McAuliffe got 48.6 percent, the second-highest losing percentage in the two-party era. Youngkin won only by managing to be sufficiently pro-

Trump to the MAGA constituency yet sufficiently distant from the former president to engender support, if only for one election, from those leaning Republican voters who stayed home or cast a protest Democratic vote in the last gubernatorial election.

Youngkin Republicans surged to the polls beyond the most optimistic GOP forecasts. But Democrats were not equally eager to vote. Publicly and privately, Democrats blame a steep decline in President Biden's approval rating, owing to Congress's inability to pass his "Build Back Better" legislation. Virginia's gubernatorial elections have historically been sensitive to presidential performance rating. But the data demonstrates that blaming Biden is merely a convenient excuse. His woes did not cause McAuliffe's defeat. Election returns bear out one statistical fact: Black voters were not enthusiastic about supporting the Democratic ticket this year.

I submit the following take, admittedly different than the conventional wisdom.

Wilder's blunt criticism of McAuliffe and Democratic Party leaders tells me he seemed to believe Democrats played the race card to stop a Black candidate from being nominated for governor this year. Wilder has been cool to Democratic gubernatorial candidates before. But this time, he did not mind if his criticism helped Youngkin win. The case for my conclusion starts with the destruction of Lieutenant Governor Justin Fairfax, the second Black Democrat to win statewide office. The northern Virginian seemed certain to become the state's second African American Governor. He had the best launching pad. Lieutenant Governors Dalton in 1977, Robb in 1981, Wilder in 1989, Kaine in 2005 and Northam in 2017 all went on to become governor. Those lieutenant governors failing to become governor were stopped by sitting attorneys general either for the nomination or in the general election.

Wilder had mentored the much younger Fairfax. Then came bombshell number one in early 2019: medical student Ralph Northam had been photographed at a school party wearing a KKK hood. Or had he? The hood hid the face. Northam was not sure, a fascinating revelation. Many Democrats assumed the worst and demanded he resign. Northam seemed ready to, which would make Fairfax the governor. It further meant the constitutional provision prohibiting a Virginia governor from seeking a second consecutive elected term would not apply in 2021. Richmond mayor Levar Stoney, a McAuliffe protégé, had been boasting about running for governor in 2021. He had neither the stature nor the résumé to defeat an incumbent Governor Fairfax.

Then bombshell number two: with Fairfax preparing to become Governor, the internet went viral when a woman, then another, charged Fairfax with forcing nonconsensual sexual activity. Fairfax denied the charges. The women never produced any corroborative evidence. Virginia Democratic leaders, allies of McAuliffe, citing the "always believer the accuser" motto of the #MeToo movement, demanded Fairfax resign. Within a fortnight, he lost any chance to win the 2021 gubernatorial nomination. Attorney General Mark Herring, facing a racial scandal of his own, found no support for a gubernatorial run.

Suddenly, the Democratic Party faced the same dilemma as the GOP: neither had a sitting statewide elected official ready to run for governor in 2021. McAuliffe tried to run for president in 2020. But he garnered no credible support. He later tried but failed to find support for a high-profile position in the Biden administration.

This left one attainable politically powerful position: governor of Virginia. Fairfax believed Stoney had been involved in leaking the initial sexual allegation. The leak appears to trace back to the wife of one of Stoney's top appointees, Thad Williamson, who encouraged Fairfax's first accuser to come forward based on allegations from nearly twenty years earlier. McAuliffe and Stoney, along with their posse, strongly deny any involvement, as does Northam's team. Yet Fairfax's troubles took pressure off Northam to resign.

Wilder surely knew what I knew: the Democratic Party establishment never wanted Fairfax to be the 2021 gubernatorial nominee. Now he had been eliminated—although Fairfax foolishly ran in the gubernatorial primary, finding meager support. The best way to give the Democratic Party establishment four more years on the government gravy train remained obvious: return the godfather, Terry McAuliffe, to power. Yogi Berra's famed adage seemed appropriate: some things are too coincidental to be a coincidence.

Fairfax's demise, the racial protests in 2020 and McAuliffe's weak polling numbers convinced state senator Jennifer McClellan and delegate Jennifer Carroll Foy to run for governor. Both are Black women. No Black woman had ever been elected governor anywhere in America. Thirty-two years after Wilder made history, Democrats could do it again.

But instead of running against his Democratic opponents, McAuliffe kept his fire on Trump and Chase. This was consistent with his running as a "national Democrat." It seemed no different than the anti-Trump campaigns being run around the country.

Yet I believe Wilder saw something else in this strategy. Seven Democrats had been elected governor in the two-party era. Five had previously won a statewide campaign. Mark Warner had been state party chair and previously ran a credible race for the U.S. Senate against incumbent John Warner. McAuliffe won but only after first losing a statewide primary run. No white state senator or delegate had gone directly to the Governor's Mansion. Why should Democrats bet the farm on a Black General Assembly member given the political stakes?

McAuliffe won 62.1 percent of the primary vote, the greatest percentage in a competitive gubernatorial primary since passage of the Voting Rights Act of 1965. Foy got 19.8 percent, McClellan a mere 11.8 percent and Fairfax barely 3.6 percent. McAuliffe easily carried the Black vote.

Admittedly, he had the powerful advantages available to a popular former governor, even support from key members of the Black Caucus. The theory that "white privilege" won the nomination for McAuliffe, or some form of racial prejudice derailed the two female legislators, is not supported by the voting data. Had candidates Foy, McClellan or Fairfax looked like McAuliffe, he would have still won in the same landslide.

Yet there was an undeniable "white advantage" or, if you prefer, a "Black disadvantage" element to McAuliffe's strategy of using fear of Chase. McAuliffe subtly asked Democrats a question they did not realize had been asked and thus did not realize they were answering: to wit, do you really want to trust a Black woman to keep Trumpism out of the Governor's Mansion?

Wilder, in my view, noticed the nuance. First, the McAuliffe team destroyed Fairfax. Then they used race against two Black women. Wilder seems to feel a race card had been played, a line crossed. A Black woman had never been given a chance to be governor of Virginia or to hold any other statewide office. This is historically due to discrimination by white male politicians. Thus, neither McClellan nor Foy could have run as a former governor with a former governor's campaign advantages. Wilder seems to feel McAuliffe put the two women in a political catch-22. I think, as a strategy matter, he is onto something.

Wilder then kept up, from primary day to Election Day, the rhetorical drumbeat suggesting the "Black" candidates for the Democratic nomination had been treated unfairly. He further questioned McAuliffe's commitment to key issues important to the Black community. He knew these comments would hurt McAuliffe.

During the runup to Election Day, Democratic leaders pointedly said Black voter turnout would determine McAuliffe's fate. Wilder understood.

Black voter turnout as a percentage of the overall electorate in 2021 fell far short of what Democratic analysts were predicting. Had these predictions proved accurate, McAuliffe would have won a narrow yet decisive victory.

Fairfax, McClellan and Foy have not disputed Wilder's analysis. As I read the statistics, the political mindset driving Wilder's criticisms is more widely held by Black voters than establishment Democratic leaders appreciate. Wilder is right: Democrats like McAuliffe take their "white" advantage for granted. The former governor is fed up with the duplicity. He wants it to end. If that means Republicans get elected until Democratic leaders get the message, then so be it.

Youngkin won the closest Republican gubernatorial win in Virginia history. He has an opportunity to redefine the Virginia GOP in the post-Trump era. Why he won is already far less important than how he will govern. Of all his campaign promises, the pledge to fix elementary and secondary education is the most important.

Youngkin is the first non politician elected governor in the modern age. All the others were seasoned if not lifetime politicians. If he keeps his education promise, he will be a force in Virginia and nationally for years.

12

THE GREAT EQUALIZER

The Fight for Public Education

Henry Howell taught me that Virginia's last segregationist governor had slipped an anti-Black poison pill into our constitution. The great irony is that Mills Godwin's parting constitutional gift is now also operating as an anti–rural white poison pill. When did I realize my own Democratic Party would not help fix it? I know that moment with clarity.

I respected Governor Robb despite our differences for one basic reason: he seemed determined to be the most pro-education governor in the state's history. In 1966, Godwin had passed a sales tax needed to fund education, but he did not believe in educational equality. Godwin and his friends in the General Assembly talked about how Virginia needed to finally live up to *Brown v. Board,* but they worked behind the scenes to make certain the revised constitution approved by the voters in 1970 contained an education clause that pointedly did not guarantee such equality.

As Horace Mann wrote and Dr. King preached, education is the great equalizer. King knew the Byrd Machine had not wanted equal education for a large segment of the white population. To them, education was dangerous: it caused people to think too long, to question too much and especially to question the actions of their government.

King understood what segregationists and Confederates knew. There is a reason that under Virginia law, free (or "free") Black people would receive "corporal punishment…not exceeding twenty lashes" for meeting "at any school-house, church, meeting-house or other place for teaching them reading and writing" and that white folks assisting such literacy efforts could be fined and imprisoned for a period "not exceeding two months."[34] King told us that only educated people have the power to know when it is time to break free of the fallacies keeping us mired in the past. Educated people know that they can insist on their inalienable rights. Education brings light; it is equally true that segregation, prejudice and hatred can only grow in the darkness. The most radical thing any society can do is ensure the new generation receives the best possible education.

In every state, government is responsible for providing a system of public education. The rich can afford to educate their children in private schools. But for the middle and working classes, public education is the only way for most of us to unlock our potential and to not be ruled from cradle to grave by our upbringing.

The requirement to have a statewide system of public education comes not from the U.S. Constitution but from the states. The main reason Virginia enacted Article VIII, the state's first such education article, stemmed from *Brown v Board I*. However, *Brown I* did not guarantee any child a good education—or any education at all. Generally speaking, the federal government does not control school policy. Congress contributes little money to K–12 education, roughly 10 percent, as compared to state and local educational funding. The top jurists in the country considered for a whole year after *Brown I* how to remedy the violation of the Fourteenth Amendment decreed by *Brown I*. Virginia and other states had broken the law and thus needed to be made to comply. *Brown II* insisted the states do the right thing with "all deliberate speed."

Brown I and *Brown II* were revolutionary. Even the plaintiff's lawyers never believed the court would go that far. But in Virginia, the Byrd Machine perpetrated Massive Resistance preventing implementation of the constitutional mandate.[35]

THERE IS A REASON Francis Pickens Miller seemed on the verge of toppling the Byrd Machine's racist grip on Virginia in the 1949 gubernatorial primary by promising to build new school buildings.[36] Seventy-two years ago, Miller, a colonel, delegate and Rhodes Scholar, pitched education as the way out of the darkness. The people knew he was right. So did the godfather of Virginia segregation, Harry Byrd. It took all of the evil genius's tactics, fearmongering and red baiting to sap enough people of their hope.

They should have known better, but they blinked and chose John Battle for the Democratic gubernatorial nomination, at that time tantamount to election. The 1902 segregationist constitution was still in force in 1949. The document had been written to strip away the franchise from 90 percent of all Black Virginians and half of all white Virginians then on the voter rolls. The Byrd Organization could control the electorate to defeat Miller. In a 42 percent–35 percent defeat (third-place candidate Horace Edwards promised to raise taxes to fund public schools and garnered 15 percent), Miller, a truly great Virginian underrecognized today, had made his point.[37] The segregationist Battle realized he would need to address the issue of the state's shoddy public school infrastructure and memorably christened them "Battle Funds."

Forty-five years ago is when I first realized the problem with the education clause. I had not read Professor A.E. Dick Howard's books on the Virginia constitutional convention. The lawmakers did not rubberstamp the work product of the commission, but as drafters, Godwin and his commission members held great sway. Howard wrote newspaper columns explaining the various proposed changes. The General Assembly engaged in debates both in the House and Senate, lively at times, finger-pointing permitted. Over the years, I have reviewed much of Howard's published materials and the transcripts of the General Assembly debates. I am therefore confident what Howell told me in 1976 did not surprise anyone on the commission or in the General Assembly at the time the state's leaders recommended the constitution be ratified by the voters.

I had been trying to understand Howell's history. This made me increasingly intrigued by the fact that Andy Miller, our primary opponent, was the son of one of Howell's political idols. Howell's first foray into statewide politics traced back to Colonel Miller. Howell had worked on Miller's 1949 campaign and chaired Miller's 1952 Democratic Senate primary when Miller lost in an effort to unseat the godfather himself, Senator Byrd. The following year, Howell lost his first solo campaign to win the Democratic nomination for the House of Delegates.

I recall talking to Howell in his office one summer afternoon. Howell's face lit up when talking about Miller. He clearly held the man in high regard, and not merely as a politician, it seemed. Going head-to-head against the Byrd Machine and therefore becoming political public enemy no. 1 took a lot of courage. I could tell those early campaigns had given Howell a political direction not before there, or perhaps not with the same populist passion. Miller's campaigns might have been the substance of weathered newspaper stories for me, but not for Howell. Despite the losses, Howell felt Miller had enlivened something important, especially as to education.

Howell knew the Miller campaigns in ways I could never learn from books. He discussed how John Battle had tried to undercut Miller's school facilities platform. He mentioned what became known as the "Battle Funds," the candidate's historic effort to appropriate state funds to help localities renovate old schools and build new ones.

Howell described how one campaigned in those days. It was a different world in both technology and society. Segregation remained rooted in Black repression and a white caste system, which manifested itself in the appalling conditions of the state's schools and the concomitant refusal of the Byrd Machine to build enough of them. Moreover, in 1949, "separate but equal" facilities were not equal by any credible definition. School buildings for Black Virginians were constructed of inferior materials and often put in environmentally unsafe areas.

The condition of Black schools was unconscionable to many Virginians prior to *Brown*. Future Supreme Court Justice Lewis Powell headed a review of the facilities when he was a Richmond School Board member in 1953; I read a copy years later at the Library of Virginia. He said children were smart. If you sent them to an obsolete, dilapidated facility, then they rightfully assumed that the community did not actually care about their education, despite the flowery speeches. Why should they? If we wanted children to take education seriously, then we needed to send them to schools reflecting that. Byrd and Godwin and their odious conspirators surely would have known about what the future justice wrote.

Howell was born and raised in Norfolk. He valued education and knew others like him did, as well. He went to the University of Virginia and clerked for a federal judge. That he became a great lawyer surprised no one who knew him. He had been fighting the likes of Godwin his entire political life.

If Howell discussed Powell's schools review with me, it went in one ear and out the other. I was looking for ways to defeat Andrew Miller, not praise the segregationist who defeated his father. The school facilities issue did not play a role in the campaign. Only later did I realize how the school building issue served as a proxy on the issue of equal educational opportunities, the bedrock of King's dream.

What I do remember, forty-five years later, is a discussion of the Virginia Constitution's Article VIII, Section 1: the Education Clause. Senator Howell pointed out the segregationist logic behind it.

The education issue came down to two things for a governor: true commitment to equal educational opportunity and the willingness to "put up or shut up" on the issue of state funding. Howell knew the likes of Godwin had no intention, rooted deep in their bones, of ever providing the funds needed to give Black Virginians equal educational opportunity. Never.

Howell knew there was a brilliant pretext for segregationists that would be hard for many legislators to resist. It fit right into the culture of the state and was consistent with its retrograde fiscal policy—though, to be fair, the financial pretext had wide acceptance across the country in most states at the time.

Speeches are one thing—putting up the money quite another. Godwin knew he would only get blowback from the handful of legislators deeply committed to equal rights for all. Everyone who understood money and education knew, too, such as Linwood Holton, the Republican governor at the time of the constitution's ratification. Professor Howard's explanations are clear in this regard.[38]

Article VIII: Education had been crafted to read as follows:

> *Section 1. Public schools of high quality shall be maintained*
> *The General Assembly shall provide for a system of free public elementary and secondary schools for all children of school age throughout the Commonwealth and shall seek to ensure that an educational program of high quality is established and continually maintained.*

To the average voter this seems plain language: the nonlegal mind would assume it reinforced the duty to ensure such things happened. The term *shall* in the law, in common parlance, means it must be done. If citizens have a legal right guaranteed by the constitution, then the government has a duty to provide that right. Should the state not do it, then lawyers like Henry Howell could sue. Godwin knew that Howell had sued to abolish the poll tax and illegal redistricting. To mislead the public and simultaneously hamstring sharp civil rights reformers in the future, the term *shall* had been cagily tied to "seek to ensure." The Byrd mindset drafted the Education Clause to *appear* to guarantee such equality when, in legal doctrine, the language provides only an *aspirational* goal ("shall seek"). Segregationists were never going to allow lawyers the ability to sue to enforce the right of children to equal education.

As we used to say in my VISTA days in Chicago, the good ol' boys were selling wolf tickets. The only difference was that the salesmen were not the kind prevalent in the Byrd days. They were newer and more cosmopolitan. As Dr. Sabato would say, they fit in at the right parties with the right people.

Sixteen years of "all deliberate speed" had given Godwin and his advisors ample time to deliberate. Several other states went through litigation over the constitutional meaning of their education articles. The plaintiffs in those cases claimed their states' constitutions required substantially equal educational spending in all the school districts. In some, courts ruled that the state needed to develop a formula to provide greater funding to poor districts, thus necessitating either raising taxes or lowering funding to affluent school divisions. This struck fear into Godwin and others committed to maximal segregation. The Byrd men understood that in politics, it all came down to green, not black or white.

When running Howell's 1977 gubernatorial primary campaign, I did not do any research on the 1970 constitutional referendum. I felt the referendum results would not provide useful turnout information, so I only looked into it when I delved deeper into school policy years later. There were actually four different referenda on the ballot that year, all related to the proposed new constitution to take effect on July 1, 1971. None of the four specifically asked voters to approve or disapprove the Education Article. The Education Article was wrapped into one up or down vote stated this way: "Shall the Constitution be generally amended and revised, as agreed to by the General Assembly at its 1969 and 1970 sessions (except for the three proposals separately stated below)?" The three referendum questions related to letting the General Assembly authorize a lottery, allowing general obligation bonds for specific capital projects subject to approval in a referendum and permitting a two-thirds majority of the General Assembly to pledge the full faith and credit of the state behind bonds for certain revenue-producing capital projects if the governor made certain findings.

It is true that there had been years of debate on creating a new constitution. The provisions had been the subject of countless articles and commentaries, some of which included discussions of the Education Clause. But as a practical matter, as the question indicates, voters were relying on the good judgment of the General Assembly, not reading the fine print with a microscope. As a practical matter, voters had only two viable choices. They could vote to keep the discredited 1902 constitution or for a better constitution lauded by a bipartisan consensus of the state's political, business and other leaders. Indeed, few reformers with any credibility were urging disapproval.

The Education Article gave politicians the ability to tell the liberals they agreed with the goal, tell the conservatives they won't break the bank and assure the moderates they can be socially enlightened without digging deeper into your pocket. Plus, they still got to spend money on special interests first.

Question 1, the omnibus, received 71.8 percent. The other three items also passed handily, although with lesser, mid-60 percent majorities. Question 1 won almost everywhere. It received more than 80 percent in Howell's home base of Norfolk and nearly 80 percent in Richmond in Wilder's. It passed overwhelmingly in Northern Virginia. Only eight jurisdictions voted against it: that opposition was centered in rural, Byrd-backing jurisdictions that perhaps really did prefer the racist 1902 constitution.

Education did matter in the 1977 primary, but not in the context of facilities. Howell had a strong record on educational opportunity and reform, and as governor, he would have proposed a tax increase to benefit education. But he did not campaign on it. The issue did not surface to any major extent in the primary. I had told Howell what he already knew: if you propose a tax increase, then you will lose the primary, or if you manage to survive, you will get crushed in the general. I could sense that Reagan's conservative politics were beginning to take hold in Virginia even more strongly. Howell had one last shot to win the office. He would not make it to the Governor's Mansion being a pro-tax candidate.

When he fired me after the primary, one reason given in our private chat concerned criticism of me from the Virginia Education Association, specifically, and liberal forces, in general, for steering him into a no-tax-increase posture. He seemed to agree with my critics. Henry said he wanted to keep the door open. We had made a careful yet accurate no new taxes pledge that contained sufficient wiggle room for what he wanted to do should he win. Later politicians would use this same tactic successfully. In fairness, we had other strategy disagreements for the general. As I have previously said, I did not handle his having fired me all that well in future years, especially after Wilder won. In the historic sense, we had built on Howell's courage, and Colonel Miller's too.

I still recall seeing Howell at one of the party's annual dinners while I was chairman. He was sitting with his former secretary, Henry McLaughlin. I did not even say hello. Looking back, I cannot imagine how I got my mind into that place. My mom and dad taught me better.

I should have made it a point to recognize that, to see Henry and thank him. I admired Henry, I still do, and I regret not telling him. Thirty years later, and it still eats at me. I deserve it. I say it now because it happened, and admission is part of the process of making change. Politics affects you; it is hard to keep your bearings and values, far harder than it looks. Howell is a giant, which will become clearer in time.

In 1985, GERALD BALILES had run on a promise. Robb had been elected as the first non-segregationist Democratic chief executive in the state's history. Robb promised to raise teacher salaries to the national average; Baliles did one better by promising to raise compensation to the national median.

At the time, Virginia had only one major dedicated revenue source for education: the sales tax. We always referred to it as the education tax. Roads had their own revenue stream, the gas tax, which amounted to a user fee. The public agreed—if you use the roads, you pay for it. There is no user fee concept for raising education money. I knew Baliles's no-tax campaign pledge had been transactional and that he always intended to break it once elected. But I never suspected he intended after his election to propose raising the sales tax to pay for a massive road and superhighway building project. Perhaps Wilder had suspected, but I never asked.

The proposal for the sales tax came as a recommendation from the transportation commission Baliles created. I believe he made a terrible policy mistake that would boomerang against education in the future. He would disagree. It was really Baliles's commission and proposal; he spent years afterward pointing to transportation as his greatest legacy.

I understand the importance of transportation for work, leisure and commerce. Even in the days of the Byrd Machine, the gas tax as a user fee to pay for roads enjoyed broad support across the political spectrum from citizens opposed to any general tax. But there is not an equal right to transportation opportunities in the Fourteenth Amendment; we did not fight the Civil War over highway construction. A new approach may indeed make sense as the advent of more fuel-efficient vehicles and electric cars and trucks challenges the traditional notion of a user fee. Yet there are ample alternatives not predicated on gutting the dedicated education tax. The sales tax had been asked to serve two purposes; 20 percent of what had been education tax revenue is now dedicated to transportation.

I knew Baliles valued education, but there is no other way for me to say it: I always thought a Democrat would put education before transportation. Baliles had broken the code and slaughtered the sacred cow; the sales tax no longer would be reserved for education.

Lieutenant Governor Wilder and I discussed this. Once the road lobby realized they could turn the sales tax into a transportation tax, the educators would find the budget battles that much harder. Moreover, as previously discussed, Baliles's reneging on a no-tax pledge could have killed Wilder's gubernatorial hopes.

In 1993, during the last year of Wilder's term, revenues were recovering from the recession. I knew someone had to make a statewide push to raise more money for education. Virginia's public colleges are highly respected among the electorate. Wilder had proposed reducing state funding of their top-heavy administrations to help balance the budget. I backed him all the way as party chair.

I thought a sales tax increase for higher education would have the most political support among the people. In my view, the more money directed at education, the better—particularly if it was the classroom, not the boardroom. More money alone would not guarantee educational reform; it would also require a new commitment for our leaders to put education first. In budgetary terms, this would enable the state to increase K–12 funding.

My plan called for the new educational tax to be put to a referendum. I figured a big win would show Democratic politicians they were wrongly putting transportation ahead of education. It remains the only time, to my knowledge, that a state party chair has dared challenge the party to face this reality. Wilder gave me the green light to do it, but it was my call, not his, in the final analysis.

In 1994, former attorney general Andy Miller, the son of Colonel Miller who had lost to Howell, sued the state on behalf of a number of rural Virginia counties whose leaders recognized the Education Clause's anti–rural white discrimination. Wilder asked him not to bring the suit; he wanted to try to fix education inequities with funding and knew the lawsuit would give legislators an excuse to wait until the court had ruled. Furthermore, Wilder knew how the court would rule, as did everyone who knew what Godwin had been doing twenty-five years earlier. Miller lost the case in Richmond Circuit Court, but he appealed to the Virginia Supreme Court. Andy meant well, but good intentions are not enough.

The ruling in *Scott v. Commonwealth*, 443 S.E. 2nd 138 (1994), showed Godwin had done his job well. The justices found that the Constitution of Virginia did not give children a right to equal educational opportunity. The court said,

> [We] *agree with the trial court that education is a fundamental right....* [H]*owever, we hold that nowhere does the Constitution require equal, or substantially equal, funding or programs among and within the Commonwealth's school divisions.... Therefore, while the elimination of*

substantial disparity between school divisions may be a worthy goal, it is not required by the Constitution.

In 1995, after Miller lost the suit, legislators from Southside and Southwest put in a bill to fix the Virginia Constitution. It was killed in the Rules Committee, 3 to 2, with the deciding vote cast by Speaker Tom Moss.

Two decades after Baliles, Governor Mark Warner proposed raising taxes to provide more resources to the General Fund. His 2004 proposal promised to spread the burden through not merely a regressive sales tax increase but also a higher progressive income tax on the state's top earners. The GOP provided the procedural maneuver needed to pass the sales tax. I knew the new income tax would be killed, as did Warner when he proposed it. The fantasy notion that wealthy residents would be willing to pay higher income taxes had long been a nonstarter to those who had been around Virginia politics when Democrats were clawing back from three straight Republican governors in the 1970s and early 1980s. During the horse-trading over transportation funds years ago, Northern Virginia legislators famously won the option of a local income tax to pay for road improvements. Editorial writers heralded the law as a big breakthrough and a chance for Northern Virginia to take control of its own destiny without waiting on the General Assembly. Those of us who knew the state's politics dismissed the idea as pie-in-the-sky. Any local elected official proposing an income tax would be immediately sent to the hospital for an emergency head check. There remains no such tax in the region today. Warner's income tax increase got dropped.

A year before, Warner had indicated to Republican General Assembly leaders a willingness to sign an end to the estate tax. I lobbied Warner opposing that idea. The Virginia estate tax was misunderstood as written; it did not change people's tax rates but gave the state some money otherwise going to the federal government. But the GOP got a Democratic governor to sign a repeal of the estate tax, except for the biggest estates.

Meanwhile, school buildings kept getting older; the education tax less and less an education tax; and more research came out showing the negative effect of dilapidated school buildings on student achievement.

SCHOOL FACILITIES

Richmond's public-school facilities had reached a state of crisis by the mid-2000s. On average, they were obsolete a generation ago. Every year, the situation became more immoral and intolerable. Bathrooms were in disrepair, heaters and air conditioning did not work and mold made children and teachers sick. Consequently, Richmond was for many years dubbed the asthma capital of the nation by the Asthma and Allergy Foundation.[39]

Tim Kaine got this. As mayor, he used historic tax credits to finance the rehabilitation of the rundown Maggie Walker High School building constructed during the Great Depression. It had suffered from every day of its six decades of aging, but the city could not afford to fix it. Then Kaine found a way; or, more accurately, he had been smart enough to seek out some smart guys to do it.

Historic tax credits had been created as part of the 1986 tax reform deal between Reagan and Speaker Tip O'Neill in which tax credits could be earned for renovations of historic buildings. The legislation had been intended to apply to all buildings to incentivize renovation of the nation's aging building stock. Buildings that captured a town's history and architecture could be saved and repurposed for more productive, environmentally friendly uses. It was also lucrative for developers. Excellent financing could be arranged, which provided a highly leveraged deal, the way developers like it. Allowing for different state and local laws, the proposed federal tax credit might reduce the locality cost by 30–50 percent.

There was concern over past projects involving public buildings and sweetheart deals that were being used to get big tax write-offs while no actual renovations occurred. They were legal accounting gimmicks, but they engendered no public benefit, only private gain. In the most notorious example, at one point General Dynamics and certain people at the Pentagon were in an agreement that would have had America renting its own warships. To prevent such gimmicks, Congress legislated the prior use rule to ensure that public buildings were ineligible for historic tax credits if the building served the same purpose before and after development. Unfortunately, Congress's overbroad language denied historic tax credit financing to local school renovation projects.

In the early 1990s, central Virginia's magnet high school needed a new home in a modern facility. Developers Lou Salomonsky and Dan Gecker were experts in historic tax credits and came to Kaine. How did the IRS define a local school? Tax credits were unavailable under the prior use rule to renovate the decrepit Maggie Walker Richmond High School Building. But while the magnet school was headquartered in Richmond, the Richmond School Board did not have jurisdiction; the school served the region and therefore had its own board. What if an old local school was renovated and used as the new home for the magnet school? Those behind the proposed project asked the IRS about the matter. The verdict soon came back; if most of the students at the magnet school are not from Richmond, then a renovation project qualified for historic tax credits. Salomonsky and Gecker would not take their usual developer fee; this would be their contribution to the city. Both care about education. Gecker is the head of the State Board of Education, and Salomonsky teaches a course on architecture at the University of Virginia.

Leaseback arrangements allowed for the city to buy the building back from a private tax credit development entity that could be created for this project. The owners of the building might be private as a matter of law; however, they would have no control over the school and thus the public benefit of the transaction remained. The agreement set times and prices for the city to buy the building back.

This innovative financing meant the city could afford the construction. Kaine got the deal done, the developers got the tax credits and the children got a state-of-the-art facility. The Maggie Walker High School building, once an eyesore, now stands as a modern, state-of-the-art building for the Governor's School for Government and International Studies, one of the most renowned high schools in the nation.

———

IN 2005, I WAS working in Mayor Wilder's office developing his City of the Future plan. I wanted to use the same historic credits used for Maggie Walker to modernize all of Richmond's aging facilities. The numbers showed we could renovate schools for $200 million less using this approach.

Virginia had more historic tax credit financing deals than any state in the country. Virginians revere history, and masterfully crafted buildings are part of it. Before the historic tax credit deal in 1986, few such buildings were renovated. When developers consider such a renovation project, there is a major risk of discovering expensive problems not anticipated in the initial cost-benefit analysis. Historic tax credits help cushion any such costly discoveries.

The financial structure is straightforward: private developers will gladly give good terms even if the localities would be outmatched negotiating with real estate mavens. A government entity is the best lessee, a AAA tenant. Armed with leases and potential tax credits, the developer can get a great loan with the highest leverage and a minimum of personal assets at risk. Banks love lending against that kind of riskless deal. The locality would sell the rundown school to a real estate development company while agreeing on a thirty-year leaseback. The private development firm would then modernize the school to the city's specifications using the firm's funds. Everybody wins. Nationwide, this approach would have saved hundreds of billions on *construction* costs, which then could have been put back into the classroom through *instruction* initiatives.

Why not allow the tax credit to be used for school renovation? Tom Kasper, one of the top historic tax credit financiers in the mid-Atlantic, first broke the news about prior use to me in city hall. The only solution was to change the law.

In the winter of 2005, I had occasion to speak to Governor-elect Kaine. He was holding a town hall at the Virginia Aviation Museum. I drove to catch a minute or two with him to discuss trying to get Congress to apply the historic tax credit to local school rehabilitation projects. I remember asking whether he thought it was worth the fight. He did and told me to call him when he could make a difference with the Congress. Even then-Republican majority leader Eric Cantor got on board in 2009 thanks to former GOP senator George Allen. I was honored when Senator Kaine wrote that "Paul Goldman…has done great work over the years to move the measure forward."[40] I give Kaine and Warner credit. They understand how this would permanently bring a whole new level of public-private partnership to building modern schools and how in a few short years it would change the lives of millions of needy kids.

After fifteen years of pushing, the measure finally cleared the U.S. House in 2019, but that was due to a master legislator, Philadelphia congressman Dwight Evans. It seemed a perfect item for the 2009 stimulus package, but I failed to sell it to the Obama White House, their education advisors or the Democrats controlling Congress.

In my view, this glitch in the 1986 law—still there after thirty-five years— has contributed directly to the decline in education around the country, penalizing children and families in hard-pressed urban communities and rural towns alike. Rundown, decrepit schools badly hamper learning, as Governor Northam pointed out in his inaugural speech.[41]

Education in America is not doing its job, and no amount of remedial learning at the college level can change what Dr. King taught us: as goes K–12 education, so goes our civic culture. Sadly, indeed tragically, the nation's K–12 education infrastructure is considerably older. The learning indices have dropped enough that many are making excuses as to why testing is now not all that relevant. Another generation is being denied the equal facilities mandated by *Brown v. Board II.*

Roads Over Schools, Again

The powerful choose to build superhighways over schools. In 2013, Republican governor Bob McDonnell proved what I had feared: Republicans had come to see the sales tax as a transportation tax first. The General Assembly, governors, CEOs, developers and campaign donors had all decided transportation required more funds. Once again, the sales tax proved their golden goose. Democrats in the General Assembly, led by 2013 Democratic gubernatorial nominee Terry McAuliffe, were open to a deal with McDonnell on using a sales tax increase to fund major transportation projects. They even wanted to dedicate future online sales tax revenue for road building, not school buildings.

I understood where McAuliffe was coming from politically. McDonnell had strong approval ratings, though they would plummet after revelations of his dealings with conman Jonnie Williams. Conveniently, the leaks on McDonnell came after he had delivered the Republican votes needed to pass the transportation plan wanted by the state's biggest business and media interests. Moreover, Republican gubernatorial nominee Ken Cuccinelli had been a political opponent of McDonnell. McDonnell had little interest in helping Cuccinelli: it is very possible he would have pointedly refused to back Cuccinelli if the corruption scandal had not made McDonnell radioactive. Cuccinelli ruled out any tax increase, and McAuliffe saw his opening. McAuliffe had always promoted himself as a businessman's Democrat, and big road projects are like the Pentagon spending of state government.

The original McDonnell proposal that claimed to "eliminate the gas tax" (it really shifted its assessment from the pump to wholesale) as part of the new transportation tax configuration would have powerful voter appeal. People have long accepted higher sales taxes over gas taxes, income taxes or car taxes. In the end, I opposed the deal. Democrats were again choosing transportation over education.

McAuliffe claimed he had no choice. Days after having his transportation plan lauded by the *Washington Post*, McDonnell's scandal broke. He later became the first Virginia sitting or former governor ever indicted. McAuliffe gained nothing by identifying with the disgraced governor, who, in my opinion, was convicted in the media without paying attention to the truth about Jonnie Williams or the prosecutors' misuse of key federal statutes. At the same time, Cuccinelli, having misplayed the transportation issue on both political ends, no longer needed to fear McDonnell's wrath. In the end, McAuliffe won the closest gubernatorial election since Wilder's 1989 recount. A win is a win. Yet there is no evidence I am aware of that backing a higher transportation tax got any votes.

RICHMOND SCHOOLS

In 2016, one of Governor McAuliffe's closest advisors, Levar Stoney, used his connections to win election as Richmond mayor. In one poll, 93 percent of the citizens said the condition of the Richmond school buildings was poor. He ran on a pro-education platform, promising to modernize the city's decrepit infrastructure. Like most candidates, he provided no details or funding mechanism. A few months into his term, it was clear his vaunted "education compact" would not produce any results.

I did not blame him entirely. The city council and school board had failed for years to develop a viable plan. They would never do it voluntarily. The new superintendent, Jason Kamras, was all talk. These were good people, but they held the soft bigotry of low expectations that is a holdover from segregation. Let me say it plainly: how many on council or the school board take education seriously, believe in King's words and refuse to tolerate year after year the condition of the city's school facilities? Zero.

Stoney's aides told me in 2017 that he would be proposing big stuff in 2018. I had my doubts.

We needed the political equivalent of what lawyers call an Allen Charge. In this, a jury tells the judge they are hopelessly deadlocked. Before dismissing the jurors and setting a date for retrial, the judge gives the jury an Allen Charge aimed at getting them to make one last full-force effort to reach a verdict.

I called up Bernice Travers, then top leader of the Richmond Crusade for Voters. I thought that we should do a referendum, the same way we got the elected mayor law in 2003. She asked me to speak to the next meeting of the Crusade. The membership seemed supportive. Bernice also had me speak to her executive committee. They seemed interested. I talked to Marty Jewell, a Crusade member who had proven so fearless in the 2003 effort. He always liked a challenge and agreed to come on board.

This required collecting fifteen thousand signatures given Registrar Showalter's pattern of disqualifying good signatures for technical reasons inconsistent with state law. As in 2003, the school modernization charter change would need to show the Circuit Court we met the requirements of

Richmond public school facilities. *From* Style Weekly.

the law so it could order it put on the ballot in November 2017. The public would support the referendum change if it was on the ballot.

We agreed on a referendum requiring the mayor and city council to either develop a fully funded plan to modernize all the schools without raising taxes or tell voters it could not be done. If they could not, then they would effectively need to tell citizens that we would all have to pay more money or Richmond's children would continue to attend the most decrepit facilities in the Commonwealth. One way or another, the deadlock would be broken.

We had both volunteers and professional circulators. The collaboration worked, and we got the signatures. The mayor, council and school board then belittled and tried to scuttle the referendum, as did the *Richmond Times-Dispatch* editorial board. We got a lot of help from Ed Jewett, the clerk of the courts. I believe Showalter would have thrown out thousands of signatures for specious reasons if not for Ed. Cecelia Hargrove was still there, too, as chief deputy to Ed.

On election night, the public broke all records for supporting a referendum. The school modernization plan received a landslide 85 percent of the popular vote and passed in every precinct of the city. Richmond had spoken. The school system is 90 percent nonwhite, mostly kids from working-class families often pressed for money. They had been dismissed for too long by people who should be ashamed for doing it.

In his Inaugural Address, Governor Ralph Northam singled out the growing statewide crisis of decrepit school facilities.[42] He did not offer any money, but at least he did not sweep the matter under the rug.

I sat down with Republican senator Bill Stanley from Southside. I had worked with Republicans on historic tax credits and fixing civil rights issues with our election laws. Stanley understood the facilities in urban neighborhoods were tragically like what rural Southside and Western Virginia faced. Stanley agreed to become the legislative godfather to the Richmond charter change effort, as did Richmond delegate Manoli Loupassi, another Republican. The bill's major Senate sponsor, Richmond's freshman Republican senator Glen Sturtevant, is a smart guy who helped. Given the powerful opposition working in the shadows, it would take Stanley and Loupassi to ride shotgun. As the chair of the Local Government Committee, Stanley wrangled a unanimous Senate vote of approval.

Mayor Stoney and his friends in the Democratic establishment like Richmond delegate Jeff Bourne brushed aside the 85 percent vote and vowed to kill the measure. Stoney had long claimed to have the muscle in the House to kill it, or so I heard. I frankly have a hard time believing he could think it, much less say it. His replacement bill, led by Bourne, was killed in committee, and Senate Bill 750 passed 97–0 in the House of Delegates as legislators realized they could not explain a negative vote. Northam signed the measure on March 31, 2018.

Even then, Stoney and City Council refused to cooperate. The measure gave the mayor until the end of the year to develop a plan. He eventually conceded the referendum had been necessary to force him, the council and the school board to do what they should have done years ago. Stoney announced his "plan" near the end of the year: it was a few pages of pablum spelling out future bond issues that *could* be realized decades later. The *Richmond Free Press* ran my response, "Pathetic," as a front page one-word headline.[43] Council backed this "plan" 9–0, as did the school board. The soft bigotry proceeded.

In response to the referendum, Stanley created the first ever Senate subcommittee to review the continuing deterioration of the state's K–12 infrastructure and appointed me as chief cook and bottle washer. It became clear that Richmond had the foulest school bathroom facilities in the state. Stanley wrote Stoney a letter asking that this shameful situation be rectified. Stoney, Kamras and the school board promised to do it, but they did not keep their promise.[44] Based on the hearings and visits conducted by the subcommittee around the state, Stanley proposed a referendum asking Virginians whether they wanted the General Assembly to fund the first-ever K–12 bond issue, for $3 billion. Given historically low interest rates, the annual debt service would have been 90 percent *less* than the inflation-adjusted amount of money segregationist governor John Battle convinced the Byrd Machine to appropriate for schools in the early 1950s. The passage of the "Battle Funds" drew praise from educators in Virginia and around the country, and when Battle died, the *New York Times* even mentioned the Battle Funds in his obituary.[45] Stanley sponsored the K–12 bond issue in the 2019 General Assembly. He could not get a single Democratic sponsor, and the Senate refused to even hold a hearing. Senators, including the three most powerful Democrats, voted to kill it.

In 2020, I asked Senator Stanley to sponsor the constitutional fix needed to remove the anti-Black, anti–rural white school poison pill from the Education Clause. The Democrats controlled the Virginia Senate for the first time in a generation, and he could not find a single Democratic sponsor.

Civil Rights Memorial and Governor's Mansion. *Author's files.*

The amendment was given to the Privileges and Election Committee, where the members passed it to the next year by a 10–0 vote. It was killed in 2021 by Northern Virginia Democrats.

This is the history from 1949 through today.

Education is the great equalizer. King knew that. That is why they do not want certain people to get it, King correctly observed. But the fight goes on, and I am determined to get these kids their constitutional rights."

NOTES

1. Virginia State Board of Elections, 1977 Democratic gubernatorial primary. Available at https://historical.elections.virginia.gov/elections/search/year_from:1977/year_to:1977/office_id:3.
2. *Smith v. Allwright*, 321 U.S. 649 (1944).
3. J. Harvie Wilkinson III, *Harry Byrd and the Changing Face of Virginia Politics 1945–1966* (Charlottesville: University of Virginia Press, 1968).
4. Virginia State Board of Elections, 1982 House of Delegates District 88 Elections. Available at https://historical.elections.virginia.gov/elections/search/year_from:1982/year_to:1982/office_id:8/district_id:27390.
5. Dwayne Yancey, *When Hell Froze Over: The Untold Story of Doug Wilder: A Black Politician's Rise to Power in the South* (Dallas, TX: Taylor Publishing, 1989).
6. Brent Tarter, *Virginians and Their Histories* (Charlottesville: University of Virginia Press, 2020), 324–28.
7. Charlotte Crystal, "A Man for This Season: Larry Sabato Has the Nation's Attention," *UVA Today*, October 27, 2008, https://news.virginia.edu/content/man-season-larry-sabato-has-nations-attention.
8. Joe Holley and Adam Bernstein, "Anne Kincaid," *Washington Post*, April 1, 2005.
9. Bob Kemper, "Issue to Be Central on All Political Fronts," *Daily Press*, July 4, 1989.
10. Caitlin Flanagan, "Losing the *Rare* in 'Safe, Legal, and Rare,'" *The Atlantic*, December 6, 2019.
11. William Saletan, *Bearing Right: How Conservatives Won the Abortion War* (Berkeley: University of California Press, 2004).

12. John Goolrick, "Wilder's Good Likely to Be Overshadowed," *Daily Press*, May 3, 1992.

13. Yancey, *When Hell Froze Over*.

14. Tarter, *Virginians and Their Histories*, 324–28.

15. Jenna Portnoy and Rachel Weiner, "Incumbent Warner Pulls Out All the Stops as Va. Senate Race Tightens," *Washington Post*, November 1, 2014.

16. Margaret Edds, *We Face the Dawn: Oliver Hill, Spottswood Robinson, and the Legal Team That Dismantled Jim Crow* (Charlottesville: University of Virginia Press, 2018).

17. John Moeser and Rutledge Denis, *The Politics of Annexation: Oligarchic Power in a Southern City* (Cambridge, MA: Schenkman Books, 1982). Available at https://scholarship.richmond.edu/bookshelf/307/.

18. Virginia General Assembly, Senate Bill 635, 1996. Available at https://lis.virginia.gov/cgi-bin/legp604.exe?961+sum+SB635.

19. Virginia General Assembly, House Bill 231, 1996. Available at https://lis.virginia.gov/cgi-bin/legp604.exe?961+sum+HB231.

20. Virginia General Assembly, House Bill 1935, 1997. Available at https://lis.virginia.gov/cgi-bin/legp604.exe?971+sum+HB1935; Virginia General Assembly, House Bill 306, 1998. Available at https://lis.virginia.gov/cgi-bin/legp604.exe?981+sum+HB306.

21. Brandon Walters, "Salomonsky Released from Federal Prison," *Style Weekly*, August 3, 2005.

22. Moeser and Rutledge, *Politics of Annexation*.

23. John Harris, "New Member Changes the History of Richmond Club's Course," *Washington Post*, April 27, 1992.

24. Virginia Acts of General Assembly, 1998, Chapter 711. Available at https://lis.virginia.gov/cgi-bin/legp604.exe?981+ful+CHAP0711+pdf.

25. Richmond City Council Voter Districts and Demographics 2013. Available at http://www.richmondgov.com/CityCouncil/documents/RichmondVoterDistrictsDemographics2013.pdf.

26. John Moeser and Dennis Rutledge, "The Last Annexation of Richmond," *Richmond Times-Dispatch*, November 17, 2018.

27. Richmond City Council Voter Districts and Demographics 2013. Available at http://www.richmondgov.com/CityCouncil/documents/RichmondVoterDistrictsDemographics2013.pdf.

28. Virginia Department of Elections, 2000 Presidential General Election Statistics. Available at https://historical.elections.virginia.gov/elections/view/39517/.

29. Frank Atkinson, *The Dynamic Dominion: Realignment and the Rise of Two-Party Competition in Virginia, 1945–1980* (Lanham, MD: Rowman & Littlefield Publishers, 2006); Frank Atkinson, *Virginia in the Vanguard: Political Leadership in the 400-Year-Old Cradle of American Democracy, 1981–2006* (Lanham, MD: Rowman & Littlefield Publishers, 2006).

30. The L. Douglas Wilder Collection, Virginia Union University Libraries. Available at https://www.vuu.edu/library/archives-special-collections/the-wilder-collection.

31. Ellen Robertson, "Former Richmond Circuit Court Judge James E. Sheffield Dies at 80," *Richmond Times-Dispatch*, March 30, 2013.

32. Gregory Gilligan, "J. Stewart Bryan III, Media General Chairman, Has Died," *Richmond Times-Dispatch*, January 23, 2016.

33. Zachary Reid, "Longtime Richmond Court Clerk Dean Retiring," *Richmond Times-Dispatch*, December 28, 2013.

34. "An Act to amend the act concerning slaves, free negroes and mulattoes." Virginia General Assembly, April 7, 1831. Available at https://www.encyclopediavirginia.org/An_Act_to_amend_the_act_concerning_slaves_free_negroes_and_mulattoes_April_7_1831.

35. James Ely, *The Crisis of Conservative Virginia: The Byrd Organization and the Politics of Massive Resistance* (Knoxville: University of Tennessee Press, 1976).

36. Peter Henriques, "The Organization Challenged: John S. Battle, Francis P. Miller, and Horace Edwards Run for Governor in 1949," *Virginia Magazine of History and Biography* 82, no. 3 (July 1974): 376–406.

37. James R. Sweeney, "Battle, John Stewart: 1890–1972," *Encyclopedia Virginia*, https://www.encyclopediavirginia.org/Battle_John_Stewart_1890-1972.

38. Ashley McDonald Delja, "Across Four Aprils: School Finance Litigation in Virginia," *Brigham Young University Education and Law Journal* 2004, no. 2 (2004): 191.

39. Asthma and Allergy Foundation of America, "Asthma Capitals 2015: The Most Challenging Places to Live with Asthma," 2015, http://www.aafa.org/pdfs/2015_AC_PublicList.pdf.

40. Tim Kaine, "Lessons from Maggie Walker," *Style Weekly*, October 24, 2011.

41. Transcript of Ralph Northam's Inaugural Address available at https://wtop.com/virginia/2018/01/transcript-ralph-northams-inaugural-address/.

42. Ibid.

43. Jeremy Lazarus, "Pathetic," *Richmond Free Press*, January 18, 2019.

44. "RPS Behind on 'Bathroom Blitz' Project as School Year Begins," WRIC-ABC Richmond, September 4, 2018, https://www.wric.com/news/local-news/richmond/rps-behind-on-bathroom-blitz-project-as-school-year-begins/.

45. "Obituary: John Stewart Battle Sr., 81, Former Governor of Virginia," *New York Times*, April 10, 1972.

INDEX

A

Abramson, Jill 19
AFL-CIO 36, 52
Alcoholic Beverage Control
    Commission 39
Alexandria, Virginia 41
Allen, George 102, 115, 144
Allen, Ray 117
Andrews, Hunter 43, 77, 82, 87
Arlington, Virginia 26, 41, 93, 106
Atkinson, Frank 52, 115
Axsom, Russ 36, 52

B

Baker, Donald 60
Baliles, Gerald 45, 57, 63, 65, 81, 95
  education funding 139
  fiscal policy 80, 83
Baskerville, Viola 122
Battle, John 134, 149
Benedetti, Joe 106
Best Products 20
Bill of Rights 101
Bliley, Tom 107, 111, 112, 115, 124

Boone, Ray 108, 117
Bourne, Jeff 148
Bridge, Chris 78
Brown, Michael 48, 69
Brown, Mike 52
Brown v. Board of Education 19, 36, 91,
    132, 141, 144
Bryan, John Stewart III 117
Bush, George H.W. 68, 79
Bush, George W. 113
Byrd, Harry 10, 31, 42, 104
  and education 133
  pay as you go policy 80
Byrd, Harry, Jr. 29
Byrd Machine 10, 15, 16, 23, 27, 32,
    38, 49, 53, 55, 64, 94, 106, 132
  and anti-Semitism 89
  and education 133
  and Larry Sabato 52

C

Caddell, Pat 66
Cantor, Eric 110, 144
Carter, Jimmy 17, 20, 41, 45, 66, 94

Chaney, Goodman and Schwerner 14
Charity, Ron 18
Charlottesville, Virginia 24, 52
Chesterfield, Virginia 44, 108, 112, 114, 120
Chichester, John 53
civil rights 10, 15, 19, 23, 36, 53, 56, 65, 105, 123, 148
Clinton, Bill 62, 73, 96
Coleman, Marshall 75, 79, 115
Cornwell, Patricia 99
Country Club of Virginia 108
Cranwell, Dickie 53, 81, 87, 98
Cuccinelli, Ken 145

D

Dalton, John 11, 12, 16, 21, 28
Davis, Dick 34, 37, 45, 52, 78, 96
Dawkins, Maurice 63
Dean, Bevill 118
Diamonstein, Alan 53
Doak, David 34, 78
Dominion Energy 11, 19, 101, 119
Donilon, Mike 61, 63, 66, 74
Durrette, Wyatt 78

E

Edds, Margaret 54, 60
Equal Rights Amendment 10, 19, 38, 39, 41

F

Fairfax County 32, 41, 65, 78, 93
Falwell, Jerry 65
Farrell, Tom 101
Ferraro, Geraldine 47
First Families of Virginia 55
Fisher, Joe 45
Fishman, Elise 14, 17

Florio, Jim 71
Ford, Gerald 41
Framme, Larry 78, 95, 96
Fraternal Order of Police 53, 58

G

Gartlan, Joe 97
Gecker, Dan 143
Geroe, Ken 98, 100
Gilmore, Jim 61
Ginsburg, Ruth Bader 103
Godwin, Mills 16, 49, 89, 94, 132, 134
  and education 135, 140
Governor's Mansion 11, 77, 83, 84, 85, 102, 138
Greer, Frank 62, 65, 68
  "Rise Above" 74
Gregory, Roger 48

H

Hall, Frank 106
Hargrove, Cecilia 119, 147
Harrison, Edie 40, 47
Henderson, Rita 109
Henrico, Virginia 120
Hill, Oliver 23, 105, 136
Holton, Linwood 44, 60, 61, 94, 136
Howard, A.E. Dick 134
Howell, Henry 12, 22, 23, 24, 28, 36, 41, 46, 47, 48, 55, 101, 140
  and Chuck Robb 78
  and Edie Harrison 38
  and educational equality 132, 136, 138
  and Larry Sabato 52
  and Tom Moss 38
  campaign flights 43
  versus anti-Semitism 89
  versus white supremacy 93
Hughes, Melvin 119

Humphrey, Hubert 94
Hunton Andrews Kurth 115

J

Jackson, Jesse 123
Jackson, Stonewall 14
James River 36, 108
Jewell, Marty 111, 121, 146
Jewett, Ed 118, 147
Jim Crow 49, 69
Johnson, Lynda Bird 24
Johnson, Lyndon 14, 24
Jones, Dwight 106, 123
Jones, Ruth 34

K

Kaine, Tim 106, 124, 143
Kamras, Jason 146, 148
Kasper, Tom 144
Kennedy, Jack (VA) 97
Kennedy, Robert 10
King, Martin Luther 49, 94, 132,
    133, 135, 144, 146, 150
Kling, Kenny 41

L

Lafayette, Laura 62, 66, 69, 74, 84
LeBlanc, Danny 36, 52
Lechner, Ira 55
Lee, Robert E. 14
Lewis, Sidney 20, 89
Library of Virginia 116, 135
Long, Jenny 9
Lost Cause 49, 101
Loupassi, Manoli 148
Lynch, Bob 120

M

Maggie Walker Governor's School
    142

Marcus, Boyd 52, 110, 117
Marshall, George 104
Marshall, Thurgood 23
Marsh, Henry 53, 105, 108, 112,
    115, 119, 121
Martin, Darryl 78
Mary Baldwin University 102
Mary Munford Elementary 91, 109
McAuliffe, Terry 145
McDonnell, Bob 145
McGovern, George 18
McGuireWoods 110, 115
McLaughlin, Henry 138
McLean, Virginia 24
Miller, Andrew 11, 16, 20, 24, 95,
    135, 138, 140, 141
  U.S. Senate race 44
Miller, Francis Pickens 32, 134
Milliken, John 60
Moeser, John 112
Mondale, Walter 45, 47
Mosely, Alonzo and Velma 13
Moss, Tom 22, 38, 45, 46, 47, 54, 56,
    98, 141

N

National Abortion Rights Action
    League (NARAL) 66, 70
National Organization of Women 39
Newport News, Virginia 26, 36, 63
New York Times 19, 58, 149
Nixon, Richard 41, 94, 95
Norfolk, Virginia 22, 26, 38, 42, 46,
    52, 78, 93, 106, 135, 138
  politics 38
Northam, Ralph 144, 148

O

Obama, Barack 62, 76, 144
Obenshain, Richard 41, 44

P

Pantele, Bill 123
Parris, Stan 64
Petts, Dave 61, 63, 67, 69, 74
Phillips, Conoly 42, 43
Pickett, Owen 27, 30, 36, 37, 57, 98
Pulley, Dick 36, 52

R

Rainey, Gordon 115
Reagan, Ronald 26, 27, 41, 44, 68,
    78, 79, 138, 142
Rhodes Scholarship 17, 133
Richmond Circuit Court 116, 118,
    140, 146
Richmond City Charter 106, 109
Richmond Crusade for Voters 28,
    146
Richmond Elected Mayor
    Commission. *See* Wilder-Bliley
    Elected Mayoral Commission
Richmond Free Press 108, 117, 148
Richmond News Leader 20, 21
Richmond Registrar 109, 118
Richmond School Board 135, 142,
    146
Richmond Times-Dispatch 10, 20, 50,
    62, 74, 85, 112, 115, 117, 122,
    147
Richmond v. United States 112
Robb, Chuck 23, 24, 26, 29, 37, 45,
    46, 51, 63, 65, 70, 78, 132, 139
  and Henry Howell 78
  and Wilder lieutenant governor
    campaign 54, 57
Roberts, Corey 78
Robertson, Pat 42, 65
Robinson, "Doc" 28
Roe v. Wade 19, 61, 66
Rose, Barry 78
Russell, Bob 102

S

Sabato, Larry 17, 24, 26, 51, 58, 73,
    93, 95, 136
  and Henry Howell 52
Salomonsky, Louis 107, 143
Schapiro, Jeff 54, 60
Schultz, Bob 81
Sheffield, James 116, 117
Shields, Tom 111, 112
Showalter, Kirk 118, 120, 147
Shropshire, Jay 85, 88, 98, 99
Southside Virginia 32, 48, 63, 113,
    141, 148
Speaker of the House of Delegates
    22, 38, 47, 98, 141, 142
Stallings, Sonny 96
Stanley, Bill 148
State Council of Higher Education
    for Virginia 102
Staunton, Virginia 64
Stoddard, George 34
Stoney, Levar 146
Sturtevant, Glen 148

T

Taylor, Elizabeth 41
Terry, Mary Sue 46, 56, 99, 102
Tidewater, Virginia 15, 26, 32, 42,
    82, 89
Timmreck, Paul 87
Travers, Bernice 146
Trible, Paul 30, 33, 37, 64, 73

U

Ukrop, Jim 119
University of Virginia 16, 51, 135, 143
U.S. Department of Justice 25, 123
U.S. Fourth Circuit Court of Appeals
    48, 102
U.S. Supreme Court 18, 61, 103, 112

V

Virginia Attorney General 11, 16, 42, 45, 56, 64, 78, 95, 99, 140
and VMI 102
Virginia Aviation Museum 144
Virginia Beach 12, 17, 30, 65, 80, 96
Virginia Commonwealth University 114
Virginia Constitution 11, 25, 39, 49, 135, 141
Education Clause 132, 135, 140, 149
Virginia Democratic Central Committee 23, 30, 44, 95
Virginia Democratic Party 9, 15, 24, 45, 47, 52, 95
Virginia Education Association 11, 36, 39, 138
Virginia General Assembly 10, 25, 26, 28, 29, 38, 40, 92, 96, 99, 141, 145, 149
and Education Clause 134, 137
and VMI 101
rainy day fund 84, 88
Richmond Elected Mayor Law 108, 109, 122
Virginia House of Delegates 22, 30, 38, 39, 56, 106, 134, 148
rainy day fund 81
Virginia Military Institute 101
Virginia, Northern 26, 27, 29, 32, 36, 39, 41, 45, 64, 65, 78, 97, 106, 138, 141, 150
Virginia Opera Association 38
Virginia Union University 116
Virginia Way, The 95
Virginia Women's Institute for Leadership 103
Voting Rights Act 19, 24, 29, 110, 113, 114, 123

W

Wallace, George 94
Wall Street Journal 84
Warner, John 29, 41, 44, 53
Warner, Mark 60, 69, 93, 141
VA Democratic Party chair 100
Warren, Earl 91
Washington Post 29, 50, 57, 71, 84, 145
Webster v. Reproductive Health Services 61, 71, 76
Wilder, Doug 28, 106
and Mark Warner 60
and VMI 102
education funding 139
gubernatorial administration 77
gubernatorial campaign 60
lieutenant governor campaign 48
Richmond mayoral referendum 118, 123
VA Democratic Party chair 95
Wilder-Bliley Elected Mayoral Commission 107, 110, 114
Wilder, Larry 49
Wiley, Bill 78
William & Mary 42, 58
Williams, Jonnie 145
Womack, Pam 98
Woodrum, Chip 53

Y

Yancey, Dwayne 48, 57
Youngkin, Glen 125–131

ABOUT THE AUTHOR

Hailed by the *New York Times* as part of "a major revolution in racial politics in America" for running the pathbreaking campaigns of Governor Doug Wilder, Paul Goldman has served on the leading edge of Virginia politics for decades.

Mr. Goldman has waged a series of historic battles to "keep the big boys honest," beginning with managing Henry Howell's legendary gubernatorial run in the 1970s into the anti-establishment chairmanship of the Virginia Democratic Party in the 1990s and through 2020's successful fight for Richmond Public Schools against the Dominion Coliseum.

Along the way, Mr. Goldman has been an uncompromising defender inside and outside the halls of power for racial justice, women's rights and voting rights, workers, the environment and the poor. Other than helping break America's four-hundred-year-old color barrier and the birth of his son, his proudest achievement has been his work to realize Dr. King's dream of equal educational opportunity for all children.